What others are saying about this book:

"Totally entertaining! This is an insider's perspective on a really cool sport. You'll love this book even if you never thought you'd try it."

Ron Semiao, Director of Programming, ESPN2
Creator of the X Games

"This book ROCKS! Half the pros don't know this stuff and should. Every luge board should come with a copy taped to the seat."

Biker Sherlock, '96, '97 X Games Gold Medalist

"Funny and informative. I highly recommend this book to anyone who wants to get into the X Games. Even the seasoned pros will learn how to go faster."

Marcus Rietema, ESPN X Games Street Luge Organizer

"In a world full of copycats, it's nice to see an authentic book written by one of the other original racers. I know. I was there."

Roger Hickey, Guinness World Record Holder

"A comprehensive job of representing what we do. The illustrations are effective and make the point in the text. Beginners will find the plans section particularly helpful. This book will do a lot to promote the sport and get people off to a good start."

Michael Shannon, Founder of RAIL-East
Webmaster of www.RoadL

D1120393

Street Luge
Survival Guide

Darren Lott

first edition

Gravity Publishing, Irvine, California

Street Luge Survival Guide

by Darren Lott

Published by:

Gravity Publishing
Post Office Box 50037
Irvine, CA 92619-0037

Copyright © 1998 by Darren A. Lott

First Edition, First Printing 1998

Cover and Book Design: Arlene Cline
Photographs: Kent Kochheiser

Publisher's Cataloging-in-Publication
(Provided by Quality Books, Inc.)

Lott, Darren A., 1961-
      Street luge survival guide / by Darren Lott. – 1st ed.
      p. cm.
      Includes bibliographical references and index.
      Preassigned LCCN: 97-95372
      ISBN: 0-9662563-7-9

      1. Street luge racing.   I. Title.

GV859.82.L68 1998   796.21
                                   QBI98-250

Survival Guide Contents

Acknowledgments

Many authors thank their parents for creating, supporting, and inspiring them. Mine also deserve acknowledgment for accepting the life-style I've chosen. They are only thankful that as I've matured, I have settled down to something more sensible like street luge. You can imagine what I've put them through.

I want to thank the dedication of my "Sportin' Wood" teammates, Dave Auld, Kent Kochheiser, and John Cazin. I am especially grateful to Kent, as he sits and reads the manuscript "just one more time," again, at 11:00 pm on a weeknight.

I am grateful to all the people who have dedicated time to this worthy sport. You will find their names and deeds throughout the book. A few that aren't otherwise mentioned are Jack Wienert, Jim Downs, and the staff of ESPN. Thanks for the great events guys.

This book went out for "peer review" and is substantially improved because of it. Content and editing thanks go to: Zac Bernstein, Jeffrey Schonzeit, Jarret Ewanek, Kelly Green, Mike Barber, Michael Shannon, Alec Schroeder, Randal Fuller, Dave Dobson, and Susannah Ernst. If anyone finds any part of the book offensive, it's not because they didn't warn me.

Special thanks to Snow. I love you honey.

Warning-Disclaimer

This entire book is structured as a disclaimer. Its purpose is to educate and entertain, not as a substitute for safe training in a controlled environment.

Every effort has gone into making this book as complete and accurate as possible. However, there may be errors both typographical and in content. Therefore, you are urged to learn as much as possible from this and other sources, tailoring the information to suit your individual needs. The author and publisher are not attempting or qualified to give legal or medical advice. If you desire advice in these areas then you should consult the services of a professional.

In this book, street luge is represented as an injurious, potentially deadly, and potentially illegal activity. The author and publisher shall have neither liability nor responsibility to any person or entity which may suffer loss or damage as a result of the information contained in this book.

The text contains graphic descriptions of injury and harsh language which may not be suitable for a young audience. Reader discretion is advised.

If you do not wish to be bound by the above, you may return this book to the publisher for a full refund.

Introduction

About the Sport

Contrary to just about everything else you may have heard or read about this sport, **STREET LUGING IS NOT TOTALLY ILLEGAL.** Furthermore, **IT IS NOT INSANELY DANGEROUS!**

Street luge is lying down on a long, specialized skateboard and riding down a paved road or path. Even in its tamest form, it's really fun. Pursued with skill and practice, it can offer both the serenity and exhilaration at which most sports only hint.

Sure, you can street luge in an illegal, unsafe manner, but then most things can be done that way. Street luge has the reputation of being an outlaw sport because of the media. They have catapulted a very few into daredevil fame while alienating a much larger group. The brave few who try based on these exaggerated or incorrect accounts find their pioneering efforts costly and painful. The only current barrier to massive participation is the spread of accurate and quality information.

What I'm writing about here is an exciting yet manageable sport. One that is equally comparable to the planet's other great adventures. In fact, I believe that correctly pursued, street luge offers the greatest "Thrill to Danger ratio" of any extreme sport available. It doesn't require highly technical gear, special weather conditions, years of conditioning, youthful abandon, or lots of money. And there are plenty of other more efficient ways to get killed or arrested.

About the Author

First of all, I'm not going to insult your intelligence by writing some heroic biography as though *National Geographic* were presenting straight facts. This book is written by me and represents my opinions. Although I'm a pro-class racer and X Games medalist, I'm not the *ultimate* authority on street luge nor is anyone else. This sport is still in its infancy and whatever we think we know may be laughable in a decade. I invite you to use my reasoning as a starting place in making your own decisions.

I began riding street luge in the late 1970s. My friend Dave Perry had put together a mini-documentary with his dad's super-8 camera. It had footage ranging from spectacular skate car crashes at Signal Hill to hand held action shots from his own proto-downhill board. I was immediately hooked.

Dave and I built matching wooden boards and covered them with shag carpeting. He showed me all the tricks he had picked up through trial and error, and a few tricks from other riders. I still have that board and use it when I teach others to ride. That it is still very rideable almost 20 years later is testament to certain lasting design principles.

On my first day riding, I smugly passed my mentor at over 60 mph and my new board flipped out from under me. Through a combination of quick reflexes, good balance, and dumb luck, I was able to stand up and "street ski" to a running stop. A good thing too, because during the half second I was actually touching the asphalt, I totally ground through my street clothes. After that, safety became paramount.

For a couple of years, Dave and I rode everywhere on every occasion; at night, in the rain, down residential streets, down sidewalks, in parking garages, on the freeway

– wherever we found an untested grade that looked faster than 20 mph.

Eventually the sport hit the "big time" with the 1980 race at Glendora Mountain Road in Southern California. There were sponsors, banners—and the California Highway Patrol. I was pictured in *SkateBoarder* magazine getting a ticket. The cover claimed we were the new skate outlaws, which became more accurate every time we rode.

In any extreme activity, I prefer to concentrate on riding the edge, not looking over my shoulder to avoid incarceration. I eventually moved away from street luge and became a rock climber, triathlete, skydiver, and spent several years as a scuba instructor.

Through all my other activities, I still kept my ears open for anyone who was still "downhilling" and of course would hear about Roger Hickey and his bone breaking death sport. I had ridden with Roger back in the early days, and he was already an established figure then. I was half glad he was keeping some media attention, even though it broke my heart that the press continued the "death wish" image.

Meanwhile, back at the drop zone, some base jumper friends hooked me up with a French TV crew doing a segment on "California Extreme Sports." They had lost contact with Roger and needed someone to "land luge" to round out their itinerary. I was only too happy to oblige. Now my skydiving rig is dusty.

About the Book

Most of my terminology comes from what is commonly used among the people with whom I've raced. "Get all of the **riders** into the truck, and throw their **boards** in the back." I like the sound of "luge pilot" but it's still trying to find its way into the vernacular. I have it on my business card and sometimes people chuckle. But I certainly prefer "pilot" to calling ourselves "a bunch of lugers."

"Luge" itself is a noun and a verb so I tend to alternate between "luge" and "board" when discussing what we ride. I might think "lean-steer gravity platform" sounds more high tech than "board." But then I'd start substituting "urethane based rolling units" for skateboard wheels and everyone would get confused.

When it comes to common usage—pilots fly airplanes; we ride boards. It's not that terminology which distances us from skateboarding is bad. It's just awkward forcing it throughout the book.

There is also some controversy as to whether the *real* name of the sport is "Dry Land Luge," "Road Luge," or "Street Luge." I suppose it depends when you started. All three terms are still in use and can distinguish subtleties in the sport.

When I started, the only "luge" was on ice. Since ice luge is already on land, "Land Luge" seems redundant. Nevertheless, it's the earliest non-skateboarding term and applies to any paved surface. "Road Luge" is a stronger distinction, referring to Luge Road Racing, and it's still in use by many "pilots."

Extreme Games creator, Ron Semiao, decided "Street Luge" is the most descriptive and has the most sex appeal. Consequently, "Street Luge" is the *de facto* title for what we do.

If you're brand new to the sport, I'll try to give you some tips on what to try first; if you're a seasoned competitor, you'll enjoy dissecting my theories (and then brag to your friends I have no idea what I'm talking about because you beat me racing last weekend). I'll try not to make too many specific equipment recommendations, because I anticipate the number of gear options will increase dramatically with a growing participation base.

Some of my recommendations will no doubt fly in the face of prevailing opinion. Like most competitive activities, the winner of the last race becomes the template for what's fast, and therefore, what's right. But with the rules and technology still in their infancy, whatever is winning today will undoubtedly be losing in the future. To avoid instant obsolescence, I'll try to stick more to what's known to work, and let the competitors build on "what's fast" from there.

Not everything is professional racing. This book will be controversial with those who think the only version of the sport is what they've seen on TV. I believe in an opportunity for people to experience the thrill of street luge without needing thousands of dollars in equipment or big name sponsors. It takes some really basic materials, appropriate protection, and a safe place to ride. It also takes the good sense to walk before you run. Any fool can buy fancy gear and go 70 mph into the side of a mountain. Be safe; be smart; be able to luge tomorrow.

Beginners will profit most from this book until actual instruction becomes available. Today, you would hardly try to learn skydiving or scuba diving without lessons. But someone had to.

The hardest thing about writing this book is to strike a balance between exaggerations on either side. We are not idiots because we use our shoes to stop. Nor can we stop from 70 mph in 20 feet. At 70 mph you are traveling over

100 feet per second; you can barely get your shoes to the ground in 20 feet. But we *can* stop really fast and are not sitting ducks for cars to run over. The pendulum swings from side to side. Let's stop in the middle and proceed with improving the sport.

I'm not going to spend a lot of time trying to convince you what a fabulous experience street luge is. Footage from an on-board camera is all it takes. I imagine you're already convinced or you wouldn't be reading this book. Or perhaps you currently ride and are looking for tips.

If you were not already intent on trying street luge, please don't let this book seduce you into something for which you may not be ready. I am going to try to present a glimpse of the dangers that the novice might not anticipate, and present contingencies for avoiding them. But I certainly won't cover everything bad that can happen, even if I *have* thought of it. And there is much more to learning an adventure sport than can be read in a book. Eventually there is training, and VERY CAREFUL practice. Even then, as I used to remind my scuba students: "This isn't Disneyland. Just because you paid money doesn't mean you can't get killed."

The Basics

Basic History

Street luge involves riding a skateboard downhill on your back. When I first started, we called it "Downhill Skateboarding" to distinguish it from ramp or trick riding. It was further described as "Laydown Downhill Skateboarding" to separate the times when you rode down the same hill standing up (not quite as fast but considerably more frightening!). Only years later did anyone start calling it "Street Luge" and now most of us welcome the change. It is less of a mouthful and immediately more descriptive.

"Butt-Boarding" was another early term for the sport, obviously named by people who rode down on their butts. Some people claim it was the very first name and historical origin of the sport.

An actual "Who's First" will never be without dispute. In the 1970s we were constantly running into little groups that thought they were the only ones in the world doing it. The sport is such a natural extension of skateboarding that even into the 1990s, guys who had never seen or heard about street luge were inventing it. I once remarked that no matter how early someone claimed to have first tried the sport, there would be someone earlier nailing metal skates to a 2"x4". Now I've even seen that in print. Among drawings of unworkable parachutes and helicopters that couldn't fly, I can imagine someone finding a Leonardo DaVinci luge design that wouldn't turn.

I discuss more history in the "Racing Organizations" section. But even a history of organizations only paints the broadest picture. We can trace some origins through the people who taught each of us. However, there are evolutionary dead ends like the guys on "That's Incredible!" who rode the Oregon backroads, dragging wooden blocks by hand to slow themselves down. They are an early memory for most veterans, but where did they go?

A search for who was first is pointless. Between regular skateboarding and what we do today there have been many technical changes. These were introduced by many different people, each one who could claim to be the "Father of the Sport." The real point is that we are all still learning from one another and that *these* are the historical good ol' days for this sport.

Basic Legality

In the Introduction, I hoped to catch your attention by disputing the myth that "Street luge is totally illegal." It is not. However, it is not "totally legal" either. Racing through the streets at 70 mph is not legal in a car, motorcycle, or bicycle; it's not legal on a luge either.

While I am not a legal expert, I can tell you that in California (and probably most other states at the time of this writing) street luge is still in the same category as skateboarding, roller skating, and other pedestrian activities. If you can skate down the street, then you can ride your luge down it as well. In areas where pedestrians are not permitted, such as freeways, you will not be allowed to luge either. If pedestrians are allowed, but skateboards are expressly prohibited, don't expect to ride.

There aren't specific street luge prohibitions yet, but Los Angeles County has come up with a nice functional prohibition. Based on Ordinance 12259 § 2, 1980 (note the year) skateboards are "Prohibited on greater than [a] three-percent grade"; meaning any interesting hill. Just in case you were hoping to play stupid about how steep the road is, it continues "nor shall any person ride on . . . any skateboard . . . in excess of 10 miles per hour." That pretty much takes the fun out of L.A. County. You can still ride legally, if you stay slow enough. Which could be useful for initially testing equipment or training someone new. I will admit though, that most people get into the sport wanting to go faster than 10 mph.

Private roads, and roads closed for the purpose of Street Luge Races are, of course, exempt. Several organizations have held races in L.A. County by obtaining special permits. That makes racing there possible, but not practicing or race testing equipment. We use neighboring counties for that.

Check the specific county and state ordinances where you intend to ride. They probably won't be so restrictive, but don't count on doing anything you couldn't do in a car. A copy of your state's Vehicle Code should be available at the local library or perhaps on the Internet. You could even try visiting your local Highway Patrol. If you are stopped by police, you'll want to be informed ahead of time about what's within your rights. If you are not riding in a reckless manner, and you have the appropriate safety equipment, they will be much more supportive of your activities.

Basic Etiquette

Which brings us to what is probably my biggest concern about writing this book. If I help inspire or enable thousands of new Street Lugers to go out and terrorize their city streets like reckless assholes, specific anti-Street Luge laws will be passed. And effective enforcement will soon follow. Essentially, it will be ruined for everyone.

If I thought this was inevitable, I'd keep my mouth shut and get all my riding in now. But looking around at all the bike lanes, in-line skaters, etc., I can see a future where street luge is also respected and hassle free; where the number of good places to ride grows, and technology increasingly improves the sport.

Because of the positive television coverage and particularly the ESPN X Games, many more people recognize street luge and are not so hostile toward it. In the early days, almost every adult was opposed to the whole concept.

We had police stop us from riding just because they were sure we were breaking "some law." They were happy to let us go the first time, but the second time they came around, they would threaten equipment confiscation or jail.

Much of the hostility occurred because we would take motorists by surprise. After mistakenly assuming they had "almost run over us" they would call the police. After a few calls, the police would feel the need to do something. If no one had called them, the police usually thought what we were doing was pretty cool.

Your main goal is **"Don't Scare the Motorists"** (or the residents). Don't even give them a reason to think they are protecting you by sending you to jail. Even if where you ride is totally legal, some frightened mother will be on the city council, and the next thing you know, "SKATEBOARDING IS EXPRESSLY PROHIBITED" on that hill. My friends and I have a policy of moving on whenever we start attracting too much attention, good or bad.

God help you if you get hurt, or worse, hurt a bystander. It is a mixed blessing that our society feels we should be totally protected. If it is obvious that you can take care of yourself then it will be much easier to avoid unnecessary oppression. But once someone else gets hurt, it will be open season.

Luge down a bike lane at 50 mph, hit a jogger and shatter both her legs. Not only will you have to live with it the rest of your life, every other street luger will answer for it also. The same goes for "spearing" a fellow rider who had the misfortune to spin-out in front of you. Going fast is only a small part of this sport. Going fast safely is what takes skill. Never getting hurt or injuring another is the measure of expertise. Keep these things in mind while designing and riding your luge.

Basic Dangers

I have considerably more miles on my bicycle than I will ever accumulate on my street luge. I am also a firm believer that bicycling is considerably more dangerous.

It's true that street luge is faster, but I'd rather slide out at 50 mph wearing full leathers and a motorcycle helmet than going head over heels at 25 mph in what amounts to a bathing suit and a Styrofoam cup. Two of my friends have experienced that direct comparison and both would agree. Had they not been wearing helmets, their bicycle accidents would have been fatal.

In-line skating and mountain biking are two other "safe" sports that I'd consider deceptively more dangerous. Not to mention skiing, skydiving, rock climbing, and other sports that are *categorized as dangerous.*

Street luge may look dangerous, but I think a lot of that is because you're already dressed for a crash. Keep in mind that when you fall, it is mere inches to the ground, and you'll probably slide, not tumble. If you are equipped for the abrasion, you'll get right back on and continue downhill. Try that on a bicycle.

Parents are worried that their children might try this sport. I'm definitely not in favor of turning children loose on steep mountain roads. Not on their bikes, their skates, or a luge. Plus, you could go broke trying to buy them kid-sized leathers and helmets every year. So they'll probably bomb your local hills on a skateboard, wearing shorts and a t-shirt instead.

Every sport has expected and realistic injuries. If you skydive enough, you may not expect to "bounce," but you can count on a sprained ankle. Scuba diving has a high incidence of ruptured ear drums, skiing has leg injuries. If you street luge, even properly, even with the right gear, you'll get scrapes. Some of them nasty, but few that should make you miss work. If you are unlucky or reckless, you can expect to break a leg from hitting something.

Then there is the unexpected catastrophe. In scuba diving, it means a trip to the recompression chamber; in skydiving, it's a trip to the morgue. Most teenagers assume that's the worst that can happen and are willing to trade an hour of fun for an eternity of blackness. I have news for them.

Before I was three years old, my dad told me why I shouldn't run into the street. He didn't explain that I'd be killed. He told me that if I got run over by a car, I'd be crippled by the curb, trying to call to my mom for help. But I wouldn't be able to because all my guts would be squashed out my mouth like a frog's. And *that's* the unfortunate truth about catastrophic injury.

If you're willing to participate in any dangerous venture because you believe the downside is painless black, then you are not accepting the True Risk. Neither is thinking you've mastered pain through body piercing, scarification, or tattoos. The very real downside is spending the next 40 years wanting to scream, but having to suck and blow on a plastic tube, spelling out "Please change my diaper!"

If you hit a guard rail at high speed, or run under the tires of an oncoming car, a long and horrific future may be your own. If you screw up badly in this sport, it can happen.

You can get into trouble by naively assuming your skills are on par with those more experienced. Fear is your natural protection from this. Unfortunately, even after you've carefully built skills and your fear has rationally subsided, these skills will eventually deteriorate. And after they do, your fear may not return to protect you. Your only natural protection then comes from wisdom and methodology.

I've taken pregnant women street luging, but I didn't take them 70 mph on a 27% grade. You need to match your skills to the conditions under which you participate. That's the ultimate criteria for any sport, extreme or otherwise. And if taken that way, the risks are minimized.

Design Considerations

There is a big difference between this book and the "common wisdom" of the sport. Most new guys start with the concept of a luge as an angled piece of metal channel and design from there. My vision is much broader.

Since street luge is laydown skateboarding, there are only two critical performance areas: The rolling assembly (wheels, trucks, and bearings); and the rider's body position. If you concentrate on these two areas, you can design an excellent board. Don't design something that looks fast on the ground but is difficult to ride. To me, **the luge itself is just an interface between the rider and the wheels**.

Currently, there are about six types of "skateboard-hybrids" you could ride downhill on your back:

- Long Board
- Wood Board
- Rail
- Sled
- Aero Board
- Skate Car

Most riders consider the **long board** and **skate car** outside the scope of street luge. The long board is really just a long skateboard, with the standard placement of wheels at either end. Your butt sits near the front of the board, as its length does not extend to support your feet. This represents the earliest form of the sport and a group of Germans currently race this style.

Skate cars are at the other extreme of skateboard technology, and yet were also ridden in the '70s. The idea for a skate car is the fully enclosed, aerodynamic missile. The rider can't use his feet to stop, so some kind of mechanical brakes are used. They are the dragsters of the sport; go like hell on the straights, but forget cornering. I remember seeing home movies of a race at Signal Hill with skate cars going out of control, rolling, spinning, and disintegrating in the crowd. In fact, many of the competition rules today are historical lessons learned from the skatecar disasters. Roger Hickey took the skate car concept and eventually created special "GF1 Gravity Cars" which don't use any skateboard parts, go like hell and corner well also. They have become a different category altogether.

Wood boards, rails, sleds, and aero boards comprise the scope of specialized equipment for street luge as it is currently defined. They are platforms on which a non-enclosed rider rolls down a sloping surface using skateboard-type wheels and trucks. Probably also included in the definition is that the rider slides his feet to stop and that he rides on his back with his feet pointed downhill. I don't know what you would call someone careening downhill head first (perhaps "an ambulance").

Wood boards are so named because they are usually constructed from a long piece of 3/4" plywood. Although they are not the current vogue for racers, they are the easiest and least costly to make yourself. **Rails** are usually made of aluminum U-channel or square stock and can be very light. **Sleds** are also commonly made of metal, and are usually the widest and heaviest style. **Aero boards** may have a base of either wood or metal and are characterized by smooth fiberglass bodies which provide an aerodynamic advantage.

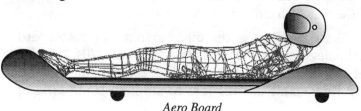

Aero Board

There are no hard and fast boundaries between the types of boards. You can build a **rail**-type board out of wood (usually called a 2"x4" board) or use riveted aluminum sheet to create a fairing. People have created 100% wooden aero boards and fabricated "classic" wood style boards out of fiberglass.

Some organizations allow all board styles to race, while others allow only metal boards of particular construction and dimensions. When all styles race together, no one style overwhelmingly dominates. Obviously, certain courses favor particular designs, but in general, the criteria for a good street luge depends on factors other than construction materials.

What follows will be a discussion of the design considerations of a good all-around luge board. I will use the tried and true design of a **"classic" wood board** to illustrate the concepts, but the design considerations should be applicable across any style.

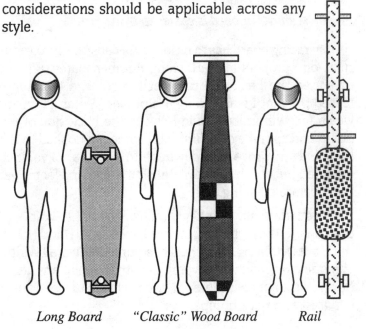

Long Board   *"Classic" Wood Board*   *Rail*

Overall Length

I'm 6'1, 180 lbs. I'll include some of my rough measurements for a basic board when discussing these concepts, but remember, the board needs to be sized for the rider. My "classic" wood board is a few inches longer than I am tall. The idea is that I can lay all the way back while my feet are on the front of the board. Rail-type boards are typically 2 feet longer.

I try to keep my boards as short as possible for several reasons:

- *A shorter board will naturally weigh less.*

- *Weight in front of the front wheels or behind the back wheels becomes a liability when turning.*

- *The longer the board, the more area to tangle with another rider.*

- *A shorter board is easier to transport.*

My racing board has to be longer because of the current rules on bumpers and attaching number plates. When I extended the back end to meet the rules, a teammate teased me that I was adding a "Spinner." What he meant was a following racer could hook to the back side of my board and spin me out. First race, someone hooked to the back end and drove me sideways into a hay bale. I've since modified the number plate extension to flex and let me get away before crashing.

There are really four key dimensions to fit any rider to their board: The distance from the **Foot Rest to Hand Holds**, the **Front Overhang**, the **Wheel base**, and the **Overall Width**. The question involving Overall Length is really answered by the other measurements, plus what you need for a headrest and back bumper.

Again, I'll include rough measurements from my own boards. Not to provide a blueprint for your design, but if your measurements are considerably different, you might go back and think through why they are.

Foot Rest to Hand Holds
(36" for me)

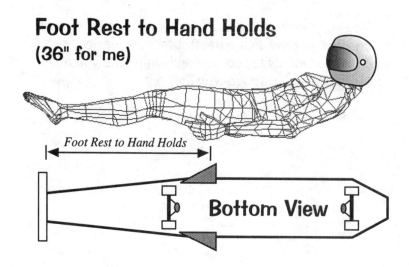

The foot rest is at one end of the board, so its placement is fixed. The placement of the **hand holds**, however, is critical within inches.

I'll call my foot rest "pegs" in most sections, because my heels drop below into open air, while only my arch makes contact. Some foot rests are designed "solid," so that your entire foot rests on top of them. A solid foot rest could be conducive to a more aerodynamic design, while "pegs" give you the quickest braking access. The following illustration shows both. When you are first learning, I think pegs are an advantage as you can tentatively drag your heels to slow, while still keeping both feet on the board.

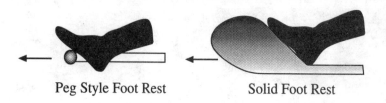

Peg Style Foot Rest   Solid Foot Rest

To decide how far back from the foot rest to place the hand holds, put on your helmet and lie back on the board. If you haven't yet attached the wheels, put blocks under the front and back end, lifting the board up to ride height. Now lift your head up so you can just see over your feet. This will be your ideal riding position. It will also really work your stomach muscles. Grab the board with both hands so that your arms can help support the weight of your upper body. Make sure you are gripping far enough forward so your arms are straight while your head is still up. This is where your hand holds need to go.

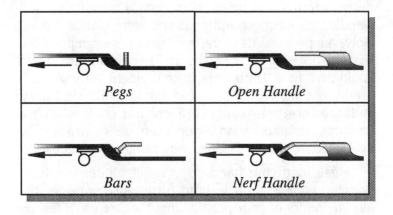

Pegs	*Open Handle*
Bars	*Nerf Handle*

Also take into consideration what type of hand holds you will attach and whether this requires further adjustment. In the classic design, I've used the wooden triangles left from cutting out the board. I've also seen plastic strips attached underneath, aluminum hand pegs sticking straight up, and lots of modified bicycle handlebars. Be careful your grips don't pose a safety hazard in a crash. I recently heard about a guy who went off the road into a ditch, stopping suddenly. He had handlebars mounted in between his legs (instead of underneath) and reportedly didn't enjoy the helicopter ride to the hospital.

Aside from your own safety, consider the safety of those around you. I think an unfortunate trend in bars is the "Knife Handle" approach. It occurs when beginners take an "Open Handle" design and make the bar ends too sharp. The open handle concept is copied from the visually beautiful Bob Pereyra/UFO design. Since it is the current template for "What a Luge Should Look Like," open handles are terribly popular. And although they look fast, I would hate to be gored by someone's knife handles in a crash. If you choose this design, think about the way you can properly smooth out the leading edge.

A safer alternative has been to carry the open handle design around and down to the board forming a "Nerf Handle." It's stronger and gives you more places to grab. However, proponents of the open handle design point out that the opening between the nerf handle and the board could become a "Limb Trap" in an accident. Although this seems less likely than a penetrating knife handle injury, getting an arm or leg caught in a limb trap could result in a bad break or amputation. Again, every design needs to be evaluated from both a riding and crashing perspective.

Make sure your hand grips won't hinder you from hanging your legs off in hard turns. Also consider the aerodynamics of your position, how secure you'll feel on the board, and where it leaves your hands with respect to the spinning wheels and speeding asphalt.

More and more, riders are bolting handle bar clamps to their luge. They slide in a short length of tube and then add the vertical "bar ends" that are popular for mountain bikes. It's a pretty clean set up—adjustability, and the availability of parts from a bike shop. Just don't adjust them into horns where they could hook another rider.

In my latest racing designs, I've gone to short pegs mounted on top of a wide board so my hands aren't exposed to the road at all. I think it has been my best design decision yet. My hands are aerodynamically positioned, and I can add push/pull forces to my lean steering. If I start to lose it in a turn, I can let the board actually tip up and skid along its side without letting go. Not only does it save my hands, it means I can recover from situations that send other riders tumbling off their boards.

If you attach your grips out much wider than your body, you will probably feel more stable and get better leverage while turning. However, your arms will catch a lot of air and you won't be able to lean over as far before hitting the pavement.

Whatever you do with your board, consider how important and delicate your hands are. Position them accordingly.

Front Overhang
(29" for this board)

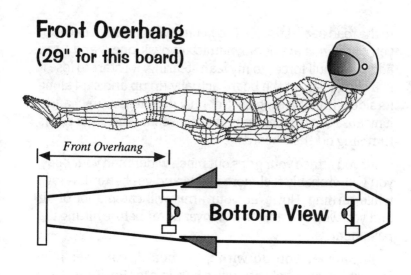

Front Overhang

Bottom View

It has been my experience that the further back you can put the front trucks, the more responsive the board. This is probably because greater leverage and weight gets applied to the front wheels, causing them to bite harder in the turns. For most riders, this placement ends up just forward of their butts. Having the trucks too far back, however, can be disastrous. I found this out when I sat up for a hard turn and the board nosed over into the street. Quite unsettling!

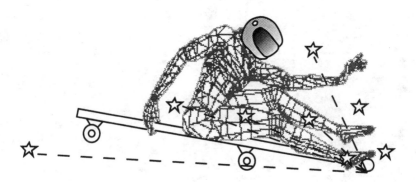

To test how far back is too far, try touching your toes while sitting up on the board. If it tips forward, you need to move the trucks forward. If you are deciding where to put the trucks for the first time, use a block in back and turn the front set upside down so the wheels touch the board. That way you can test your placement before you drill holes.

Even if your board doesn't nose over, the front trucks can be too far back for the balance of your board. Particularly if your board has a longer or heavier rear end. A front truck positioned too far back can take most of the weight off the rear wheels, allowing the rear of the board to slide around while you pivot on the front set. You can also end up overloading the front wheels, so they will slide out when you try to dive into hard turns.

On the other hand, if you put the trucks too far forward, there won't be enough weight on them, which will contribute to "queasy" handling or even speed wobbles. (See the sections on *Trucks* and on *Weight Distribution* for further discussions.)

If you are just starting out, it's much better to err on the side of having your front trucks a little too far forward. The result will probably be a more stable board that just doesn't turn as sharply. Also consider that anything that makes your board more front heavy (like a front fairing) may require resetting the trucks even further forward.

Wheelbase
(42"-52" axle to axle)

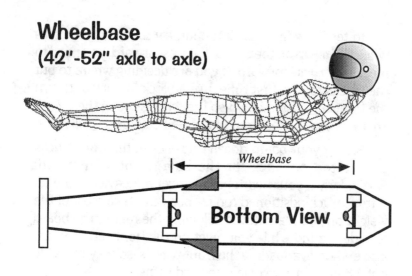

Like all wheel-based vehicles; the shorter the wheelbase, the tighter the turning radius, the longer the wheelbase, the more stable the ride. Most luge boards follow the rule of thumb: One set just in front of your butt, the other set behind your head. Is this because of the inherent physics of the sport or because we all copy each other? Let's examine some of the design constraint issues.

We've already discovered the test for putting the front trucks too far back from the front—you'll nose over. If you put them too far forward, the board handles poorly. Back wheel placement seems to be less definitive. I suppose you could move them so far forward that you'd tip over backward, but no one puts them anywhere near that point. Actually, the controversy seems to surround how far behind your head they should go.

I need to point out though, that wheelbase is where I differ drastically from the current norm. Typical street luge wheelbases are a foot longer than mine. Depending on the board design, I look to a wheelbase in the 42" – 45" range. Most other riders have between a 50" and 60" wheelbase.

Some people even recommend putting the back trucks a foot behind your head! This is supposed to prevent instability, which I'm sure it does, but at the cost of turning performance.

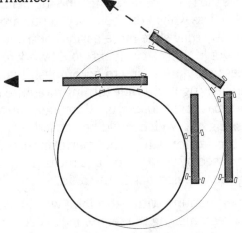

The Shorter the Wheelbase, the tighter the turning Radius

As I am now pretty confident with the stability of my board, I am always looking for ways to *shorten* my wheel base. I've started experimenting with how far *under* my head I can put them and found that wheelbase and stability also depend on the truck angles (see section on *Trucks*) and the geometry of the board. A good wheelbase falls between rear trucks that are too far back and feel "lazy" and those that are too close and feel "nervous." I think what ultimately determines an optimum wheelbase is by what happens when sliding through a turn.

The worst case slide is the drastic **understeer**. This is where the front end won't cut as sharply as you've intended and you keep heading toward whatever you were turning away from. It's also know as "pushing" or "washing out" the front end. **Oversteer** is where the back end slides around, sharpening the turn angle. In its drastic form, oversteer results in spinning out. Both types of slide result in scrubbing off valuable momentum you would prefer to hold around the turn.

As you move the rear wheels further and further behind you, there will be less weight on them as you pull around a turn; consequently they slide more easily, contributing to oversteer. You would think that riders would work to avoid oversteer, unless they are trying to accomplish two other things: [1] artificially tighten a wide turning radius (to which the longer wheelbase contributes) or [2] compensate for the front end washing out (which could be caused by placing front wheels too far forward). Both performance issues should be addressed by trying to reduce the turning radius while keeping the wheels stuck to the road.

Riders experimenting with extra long wheelbases tell me that if you keep moving the rear wheels further back, the board will stop oversteering and begin to understeer again. In this case, almost no weight is on the back wheels and the front end slides out because it can't handle the entire load by itself. So a board that understeers, can again be determined by either too much or too little weight on the front wheels. (See section on *Weight Distribution*).

On the other hand, if you move the back wheels too far forward, the back end may not slide as much as the front— the dreaded understeer, or worse, break loose suddenly and spin you into a guard rail. Experiment cautiously with wheel placement and start by setting the front wheels first.

I'll discuss turning more in the *How to Ride* section, but for now I will give you an important caveat. No matter how well you can hold a turn, in your desire to take it sharper and faster, there will come a point where all the wheels lose traction and slide. That's the main limit to how fast you can ride a twisty road. Personally, when I eventually lose traction at both ends, I want the overall effect to be a very slight, predictable oversteer. That way, the board will lose speed as it slides through the turn, but will still be pointed in the right direction when it re-grips the road.

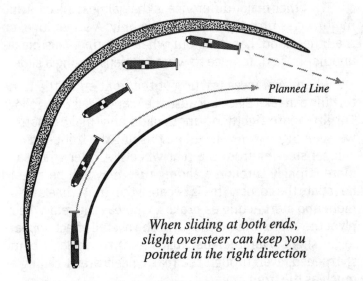

Planned Line

When sliding at both ends, slight oversteer can keep you pointed in the right direction

Conversely, several riders have told me they design their boards for slight understeer. In either case, the operative word is *slight*. Just by shifting your body weight, the end that slides more will change. This is because the geometry governing street luge handling can be tricky.

A street luge leans into a turn like a motorcycle, but rides on the bottom of it's wheels like a car. You can compensate for strong oversteer on a motorcycle by turning the front wheel toward the slide. Same with a car. A luge, however, can't steer into a slide because the direction the wheels are pointed is determined by the side to which the board is leaning. To steer a motorcycle into a slide, its rider merely turns the bars. A street luge rider, however, has to lean his board from the inside of the turn to the outside. As you can imagine, the sudden shift in weight (or traction) will cause the rider to fly off the board toward the outside of the turn. In motorcycling, it's known as a "high side." Consequently, no one wants strong oversteer from their luge.

The other major difference is that (almost all) cars and motorcycles turn the front wheels only. A street luge, on the other hand, has true four wheel steering. This makes another huge difference to what happens during a slide.

When a car loses traction at the front end, little to no turning can take place because the rear wheels only follow. Turning more tightly during a slide only makes matters worse. A luge, however, can be pushing the front end and still get steering from the rear wheels! A rider who leans more strongly through a sliding turn may still be able to negotiate the corner. This is because the front wheels scrub more and start acting as brakes, whereas the rear wheels pivot the board around the turn. The overall effect appears to be slight oversteer because the turn angle is being sharpened, even though the rear wheels aren't sliding as much as the front ones.

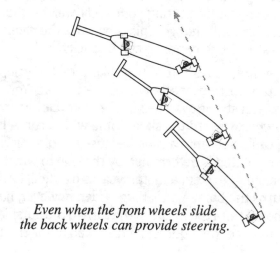

Even when the front wheels slide the back wheels can provide steering.

Evidence of this effect can be extreme front wheel wear on a board that doesn't seem to understeer. Also, a luge which has had the steering tuned out of the rear trucks will lose the advantage of this rear wheel steering. (See section on *Trucks*.)

One last issue concerning wheel base. The further apart your front and back trucks are set, the more weight between them. As the wheelbase gets longer the board between must be stronger. Your board will probably have some flex while you ride. Some flex will make the ride more comfortable, but too much flex will allow the bottom of the board to scrape. God forbid your luge snaps in half over a hard bump at speed. A good way to test the strength of your finished luge is the "Bounce Test." Stand or kneel in the middle (without it rolling out from under you) and bounce up and down. If you are afraid this will break your board, or it does, don't ride it.

Overall Width
(14" this board)

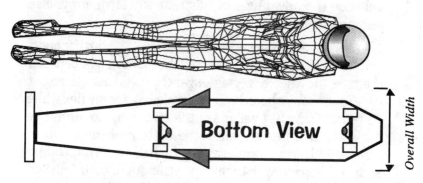

Overall Width

The width dimension is bounded by "too narrow for the trucks" and "too wide to turn". Too wide to turn depends on how low the board is to the ground, but usually a board's width is designed around aerodynamic considerations and comfort. The width of a board will generally vary along its length.

The original '70s rail-style boards were just wide enough to accommodate the width of the trucks with the wheels hanging to the outside. A wider seat immediately became requisite as no one wants to ride with a rail up their butt. The other problem with a very narrow board is the wheels tend to throw water, dirt, mud, and other debris up on the rider. The rider may also find their leathers rubbing against the wheels, inadvertently slowing them down.

I've seen fenders welded to the trucks, but most rail designs start adding fenders to the board, including "belly pans" to separate the rider from the wheels below. To let the rider sit even lower to the ground, sections of the rail "chassis" are removed, and the pan itself becomes a structural support. Thus begins the evolution of a rail into a sled.

In terms of aerodynamics, there is no practical benefit to having the board more narrow than the rider. In fact, an argument can be made that the smooth surface of the board is

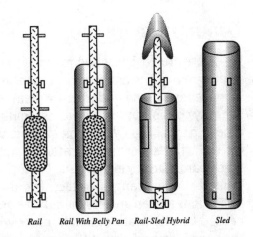

Rail   *Rail With Belly Pan*   *Rail-Sled Hybrid*   *Sled*

preferable to having a body bulging over the sides. Because of less underside drag, the theory is that at higher speeds the board can begin to glide over the surface of the road, sort of like a Frisbee gliding in ground effect.

When a board is designed very low to the ground, the extra width required to separate the rider from the ground interferes with the board's ability to lean. In these cases, the sides are bent upward, providing both coverage and ground clearance.

It also doesn't hurt to make the foot rest as wide as the outsides of your feet while in riding position. The area behind the foot pegs should be narrow enough to allow the foot to drop downward when braking.

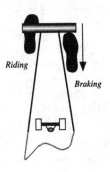

Riding

Braking

If you plan on racing, check the max width rules and make sure your board will fit between any starting poles.

Ground Clearance

There are basically two reasons to design a board low to the ground. The first is to prevent as much air as possible from being trapped underneath, creating drag. If that were the only consideration, the easiest solution would be to put a belly pan all the way to the ground, with only little slits for the wheels. For racing cars this approach works, but luge boards turn by leaning and the lower you get, the more limited the lean angle. In fact, there are three separate limitations to lean angle: When the board hits the ground—caused by this width to height ratio; when the wheel hits the board—caused by insufficient spacers under the trucks; or just the mechanical limitation of the trucks themselves. It would be nice to have a design in which all three limitations occurred at once, indicating the optimal balance between low and wide.

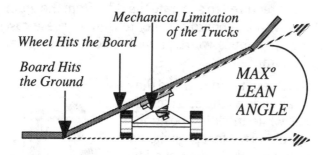

The second reason street luge boards are designed low to the ground is to maintain a low center of gravity, which should aid in your ability to hold a sharper turn. The other factors involved include: The turn angle of the wheels (which is directly related to the Max Lean Angle and the angle of the trucks), the wheelbase (as previously discussed), and the traction of the wheels (which depends on their material, the surface and temperature of the road, and the amount of weight pushing downward compared to sideways).

Many racers get carried away with trying to have the lowest board to the road. They think it is a magic formula for speed. Inevitably, these boards scrape directly against the bumps and dips in the road, more than cancelling any reduced air friction. An extremely low board can also be more difficult to turn if the center of gravity removes the leverage needed to pivot the trucks.

When you are building your first board, I wouldn't be too concerned with "low." Bolt trucks to the bottom of a flat board and have fun while learning to ride. Fighting for speed optimization can always come later when you build a racing board.

Weight

This is one of the most important elements of street luge design and still one of the least understood. Probably again because it involves balancing between too heavy and not heavy enough.

Considering wind resistance only, the more you and your board weigh, the faster you will go before reaching terminal velocity. Heavy people fall much faster when skydiving; and on long, steep grades, trucks can coast much faster. So gain weight and build the heaviest board possible, right?

Not necessarily. Heavy boards don't corner nearly as well as their lighter counterparts, so if you're riding on a winding course, all the speed you pick up in the straightaways will be lost scrubbing your wheels around the corners. Also, heavier boards don't roll away from the starting line as quickly. This means that if you're racing on a short course, you and your heavy board will be left in the dust. And in corners where everyone slides and slows down, the lighter boards/riders will accelerate away more quickly.

On a long straight grade, the heaviest boards will have an advantage, but even this is limited. Aside from wind resistance, there is the issue of rolling resistance.

Street luge already strains wheels and bearings beyond their intended use (until we can buy equipment designed specifically for the sport). Adding weight only compounds the problem. Not only by decreasing the time to failure, but also by decreasing immediate performance. I haven't done any scientific studies, but my experience says there is a Top Speed/Total Weight curve involved.

You can try to compensate for additional weight by using higher quality bearings, but our wheels continue to deform under higher loads. If you try using increasingly harder wheels, you begin to give up traction. There is only so much force you can expect skateboard equipment to handle before failing.

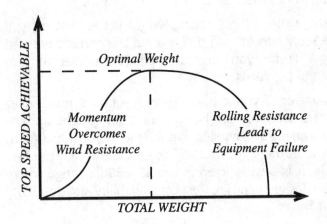

If you aren't shooting for the highest top speed, a lighter board makes sense. Lighter is easier to transport, easier to turn, easier to control in squirrelly situations, and easier to stop. Because of the difficulty controlling a heavy board, current weight limitations for racing are set at 40 to 50 lbs. This would be extremely heavy for casual riding and most racing boards weigh about 30 lbs. (with wheels and trucks attached) anyway.

Spending a lot of money on exotic materials to make a board as light as possible seems counterproductive as well. Really light guys on really light boards do well off the line, but get eaten up on the straights and particularly on level or uphill sections. So it's not like cycling where removing a few grams from your equipment makes the difference.

Conversely, really heavy guys with any kind of board don't seem particularly fast either, so I don't expect the sport to gravitate toward Jockey or Sumo Wrestler body types. It could be that even with a weightless board, the big guys would be just too heavy for the wheels. Or it could be that besides being heavier, they are larger as well and therefore offer more area for wind resistance.

I think the optimal racing weight is the heaviest you can reliably control and pull around the corners without sliding. This gives you the greatest possible momentum into and out of the turns.

However, if you are a beginner, a board much over 35 lbs. is probably too heavy. Don't get caught up into building an ultra heavy sled that will rocket you into a guard rail; or a feather-light that self destructs through the first pothole. It is best to keep in the 25 – 35 lb. range where you can design in the greatest controllability and durability of your board.

Body Angles

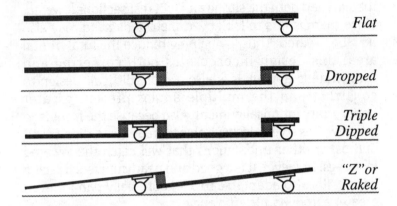

Flat

Dropped

Triple Dipped

"Z" or Raked

Most of the experimentation among racers at this time involves the body angle of the board. **Flat** boards are the most traditional and have definite advantages in some areas. I've been experimenting with a Raked design, hoping it combines the advantages of the other three. All designs have advantages on certain types of hills.

A **Flat** board is the easiest to construct and is usually the least expensive. It has the best ground clearance and does well over uneven surfaces and can do well on very curvy roads. It's flat, smooth underside is aerodynamically desirable.

Dropped boards are often designed under the erroneous assumption that lower is necessarily more aerodynamic. However, when only one part is dropped, the rider's head and feet may still catch as much air as with the flat design. If the "lower" rider presents essentially the same frontal area (albeit in a slightly different way) the real advantage of the drop comes when cornering. Because the rider's butt is very low to the front axle, less effort is required to initiate a turn and the board will feel more stable.

Triple Dipped is a term I was introduced to by the Schroeder "Fluid Drive" racing team. It indicates a board that has had both the sitting and foot rest sections lowered. Since there is less to look over, the rider's head may also now be lowered. Thus, by helping reduce the total frontal area, this design incorporates both cornering and aerodynamic appeal. It is also a more difficult design to construct and the multiple angles present greater opportunity for misalignment. Also because the front is so very low, this style is less suitable for roads with dips, speed bumps, or other undulations that will catch the lowered foot pegs. However, it is a good and nearly universal racing design. It's also adaptable to a smooth belly pan for even greater aerodynamic efficiency.

Raked is a style I began using while trying to improve on the Triple Dipped boards. It has both the advantages and disadvantages of a low front end and the sitting area is low for easier turning. The construction is somewhat simpler in that there are two less sets of hard angles. However, it's more difficult to set up because the geometry changes with the placement of the trucks. The "Z" board design was experimented with and abandoned in the late '80s. I first heard about them after I brought my "new invention" to the first race. "Z-Board. Yeah. We tried that about 10 years ago. Doesn't work."

Fortunately, reinventing occasionally means the original mistakes aren't carried over. I hoped so in my case. The secret lies not simply in the angles, but in the wide, raked body sections. My theory is that raising the rear section does not increase frontal area since the rider's head is up anyway. Same with the rise from foot rest to the hips. Since the top of the rider/board presents the same area to the wind, if the bottom isn't aerodynamically worse, the board should do as well as other styles.

The hopeful advantage of the Raked Style is that higher pressure air created at the front drop will be pulled back in by the raised rear. Sucking the air back in should help ruin the draft that so many have exploited just before passing me. Over the last few years I have noticed riders who would draft and pass my "Flat" board, now can't draft the "Rake." After setting top qualifying times and winning several medals, other racers have become interested in my "new" design. One way or another, this design "sucks."

Stress Points

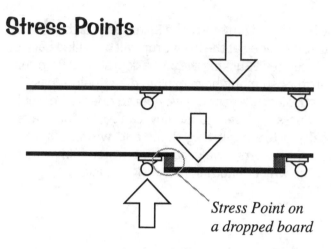

*Stress Point on
a dropped board*

A flat board will be weakest at the mid point between the wheels. It's where you will get the most flex out of the board, and it gets weaker as you extend the wheelbase. However, your body position will place most of your weight up toward the front trucks, where it is largely supported by the front wheels themselves. So there is less chance that a flat board will break while riding it.

A dropped board (regardless of construction material) will have a different set of stresses. The weight of the rider pushes downward at the front of the seat, with the opposing force pushing upward from the front wheels. The result is tremendous strain at the dropped joint. If your board is going to break in half, this is where it will happen.

Metal dropped boards use strong welds and/or gussets to beef up this joint. Wood boards need to be frequently checked for any signs of delamination or cracks here. Because it is more flexible, a failing wood joint will probably start by splitting and sagging. The rigid nature of metal will probably mean the joint comes apart all at once. Regardless of material type, it's a pre-ride inspection item.

Front Ends

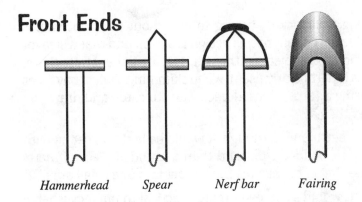

Hammerhead   Spear   Nerf bar   Fairing

There are four different types of front end treatments. A type currently in vogue is the pointiest and also the most pointless. These are called "Spear" boards because the only purpose of their design is to spear a fellow rider who has been unlucky enough to fall in front of one. I don't mean that anyone is actually building this style to hurt other riders; some of my best friends have ridden Spear boards. But I think some people might think they look faster, and haven't thought about the potential for hurting someone else. I'm hoping this book will help raise awareness of this issue before there are memorable cases of actual injuries.

At recent races I have been happy to see everyone working together to make sure all of the boards have padding over sharp angles. And in case anyone is wondering, a sharpened protruding front end does not make the board any more aerodynamic. The little bit of wind effected by the point immediately slams into the rider's feet anyway. If anything, the additional weight ahead of your wheels only helps to pull out the front end during turns.

In the interests of safety, more organizations are requiring a rubber bumper on the front and back of boards. They may also require a "nerf bar" which typically involves using flat stock or tubing to round out the front end. A potential benefit of this design is a front end that will favor glancing off objects rather than trying to penetrate them. This is particularly useful when skimming against hay bales during a race. Exposed pegs want to catch and draw you into the hay.

Keep in mind, though, it would be better to get hit with a large, padded front end than a rounded piece of metal tube that concentrates the impact into one small area.

It would seem even more practical to put a crushable fairing over the front end. Some races disallow fairings; however, if you're not racing in one, you can sport whatever front end turns you on. Implemented correctly, a front fairing can really improve your top speed. But keep in mind, a badly designed fairing will hurt performance; not just speed, but handling as well. The extra weight in front always extracts a turning penalty, and at high speed, directing the air incorrectly can make your ride very unstable, or even dangerous.

I'm sure someone soon will start marketing prefabricated front fairings. The benefit will be less trouble for less cost, and I'll bet they'll be designed properly. A fairing could be made of plastic covered Styrofoam, like a bicycle helmet, so it would be light and inexpensive. A rider would have several on hand, so when they crashed and destroyed one, they could just fit another on to their otherwise undamaged luge. Racers should like it, because its a good area to display a racing number and sponsor decals. Spectators would like it, as the front of the board is the first thing they see as racers come down a hill. I can imagine someone introducing a product line that includes a separate front fairing that you could attach to a board of your own (or someone else's) design.

I have had other riders tell me that having a metal spear several inches in front of their feet would help absorb the impact of a crash. This "Crumple Zone" thinking is a good idea, but is not implemented in the way they think. A large metal rail in front of your footpegs will not absorb the crash. In fact, because of the rigid nature of the material, all of the force will be transferred through the footpegs into your arches. In a heavy impact you will minimally break your feet.

Think of it this way – if you jumped off your roof, would you rather land with both feet on the driveway (ouch!), or onto a narrow metal pipe 5 inches above the driveway (double ouch!!)? The most practical way I can think of to implement a street luge "crumple zone" is again the large foam front end. (Hey, what about a hollow one that has an air bag inside?)

When I'm not riding with my homebuilt Styrofoam fairing, or my "race-legal" nerf bar, I prefer a "Hammerhead" approach to my designs. It's very easy to pad (using inexpensive pipe insulation), easy to construct (using aluminum angle), and doesn't put any weight unnecessarily far away from the front wheels. It also makes the board easy to stand on either its nose or tail without damage. It keeps the overall length down to help with turning (and loading the board into a car) and distributes any frontal impact over a larger area. If I crash into something, the aluminum angle bends back, absorbing some of the impact. I throw the bent one away, and replace it with one of the pre-drilled spares I carry. Retape the thick foam pipe insulation and I'm ready to roll. I've never hurt another rider, and the myriad curbs I've hit haven't destroyed my boards either.

Seat

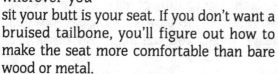

Wherever you hang your hat is home; wherever you sit your butt is your seat. If you don't want a bruised tailbone, you'll figure out how to make the seat more comfortable than bare wood or metal.

The style that defined a generation came from the Bob Pereyra/UFO Sports connection. Ron Amos, the other half of UFO sold a lot of boards of this style, including to the top finishers at the '96 X Games. Consequently, several other small manufacturers copied the style, which became known as "UFO clones."

If imitation is the sincerest form of flattery, Bob should feel very flattered. The modular guitar shaped seat with integrated open handles makes an otherwise undistinguished piece of channel look fast. It isn't functionally unique, so no one can claim to have discovered it independently. It just looks really cool.

When you design your own seat, don't feel compelled to copy someone else's style. Concentrate instead on how it works. Is it durable? Is it comfortable? Is it easy and inexpensive to make? Does your seat cover bolts you'll need to get to later?

You may originally want a seat that prevents you from slipping around. Later, when you discover you can shift your hips to set up a turn, you'll want a surface that isn't too grippy. A material that absorbs vibration can also be a big plus. A comfortable seat reduces rider fatigue and a relaxed rider will be able to turn more fluidly.

Headrest

In the early days, Dave Perry and I built headrests to help our stomach muscles last. These days, a proper headrest is a prerequisite to winning races.

Wait until your board is all done before you try to design a headrest. Then lie down and have a friend place objects between your helmet and the board to achieve the desired height.

When you're first starting out, design a headrest that will give you comfort and visibility. And don't make it too wide. Make sure you can easily lean your helmet side to side.

Foam and duct tape are excellent materials from which to build a headrest. You can make a little base of wood and then add foam and tape until you build it up to the right height. After you get the dimensions correct for your board and helmet type, you can have it covered with fabric or vinyl to make it look more professional.

Headrests are important for racing. You need to get your head as low as possible for better aerodynamics but you still must be able to see. You can get your head the lowest by using a headrest because it pushes up on the back of your helmet. This enables you to lean all the way back while the headrest tips your helmet forward so you can see. The result is that your head is even lower than you can accomplish with muscle control alone.

If you don't build a headrest, you'll still be fine for short roads. However, as the runs get longer, you'll start sitting up more and more, and start supporting your head with your hands.

Fasteners

Metal boards are usually welded while wood boards use a combination of screws and glue. In either case, the bonding areas should end up stronger than the materials themselves. However, if you plan to take any part of your luge apart, you'll be using fasteners to bolt things together.

When I started, I was a knucklehead teenager and scrounged up parts to put my luge together. Any mishmash of screws that would fit through the base plate got used. Metric, SAE, Phillips head, slot screws, different thread pitches—we didn't even have lock nuts at first. We rarely had all the tools needed to tighten things because everything was a different size. And of course everything vibrated loose and screws would get bent. The trucks never fell off the board, but working on it was a pain.

As soon as I got a little smarter, I became emphatic that all the screw heads matched. **Nylock nuts only.** Extra replacements for everything. And here is another tip. Stock several sets of your mounting fasteners in various lengths. Bring them with you. Changing a wheel size can mean adding or removing riser pads, which will mean the current screws are now the wrong length.

Also, be careful about thread pitch. Both 10-24s (coarse) and 10-32s (fine) will fit through most base plates. They look almost identical. BUT THE DAMN NUTS CROSS THREAD BETWEEN THE DIFFERENT PITCHES. That's really fun when you're sitting in the dirt trying to make changes by the side of the road. I no longer want anything to do with 10-24s. I made my choice and I don't even want a single one in my garage. I'm a 10-32 guy now.

Fine thread fasteners (like 10-32s) are the strongest, due to a greater cross sectional area. But course fasteners are better for holes tapped in aluminum and other soft materials. Use what's appropriate for your application.

When I first saw rules on grade 8 mounting hardware, I thought "Oh great, now I get to hunt down specialty hardware and spend extra money just so we can sound hi-tech." But I was wrong. **Grade 8 fasteners are cool.**

I never had my regular cheap-o hardware store screws break off. Maybe it's because I used wood boards and wood will give before shearing off metal. But the long screws always bent, making it difficult to take the trucks off. And then you couldn't reuse the cheap screws. So eventually, cheap screws became expensive because I had to replace them all the time. Plus, if the screws were bending, my trucks must have been getting out of alignment.

My high quality fasteners never bend and everything stays aligned. They are more expensive and somewhat difficult to find. But I like them. Actually, the grade 8 designation is for bolts only. Fasteners like 10-32s are too thin to fit the bolt designation, but you can ask for a grade 8 equivalent of a socket head cap screw, and have a really beefy way to attach your trucks. (Hint: They are usually black, but don't expect that all black screws are of high quality.)

Last tip for the wood guys. After you ride for a while, the wood under the screws will compress and you'll be able to tighten them even more. As you keep tightening, the screws eventually start sinking deeper into the wood. This could become a problem. I've used large washers which work well. **Tinnerman washers** work even better. They are very large dimpled (counter sunk) washers used in the aircraft industry. They let you flush mount screws and won't let them keep pulling through a wood board.

Finished Characteristics

After your board is all complete, it will have certain characteristics that derive from the sum of its parts. You can try to plan for these characteristics, but they are not a single easy measurement like width.

How aerodynamic you are on your board could be captured by a specific drag coefficient and a frontal area grid. But short of a home wind tunnel, I can't give you an easy way to document drag from design to design.

You could also develop elaborate jigs to measure the torsional flex (twist characteristics) at various points on the board. From there you could compile a profile, trying to capture how the board will feel. But sometimes the feel of a luge is better captured by adjectives like "solid," "mechanical," "alive," or "twitchy."

Fortunately, there *are* at least two other characteristics that can be very easily measured and help you compare one board to another.

Weight Distribution

How much weight is on the front wheels versus how much is on the rear wheels is how you measure the weight distribution for a street luge.

I think you want a little more weight on the front end to enhance controllability. However, if you have too much weight over the front wheels, the back will slide too easily, your front wheels will wear out too quickly, and you will not go as fast because too much energy is going into distorting your front wheels (the "flat tire syndrome"). And keep in mind that as you move around on the board the distribution changes radically. The baseline should be measured with the rider in a tucked, aerodynamic position.

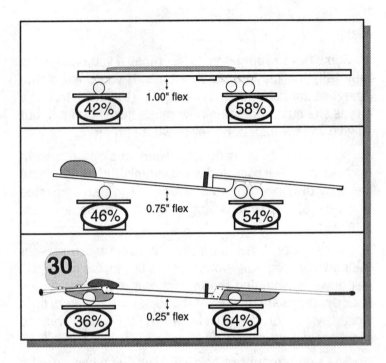

To judge how exacting this baseline distribution is, I weighed myself lying down on three of my very different boards (by putting a scale under each set of wheels). Each board was optimized for its type, based on handling and my riding style. You must weigh your board while on it for comparison and let someone else read the scales. The weight distribution of the board, independent of the rider, is not as meaningful.

From the diagram, you can compare the difference between my classic flat wood board, my wood racing board, and my metal racing board. They have very different dimensional measurements. However, it turned out that all three balanced for their optimal purposes with an average **60/40** front to rear ratio.

Flex

Some flex to your board is desirable. If you build a box tube rail, you may miss out on this. If you build a thin fiberglass laminate you may be fighting too much flex. The jury is still out concerning how much flex is optimal, but I'll give you my experience as to what I prefer.

Metal boards with no flex seem to skip around in bumpy turns. The back end will suddenly shift around and feel very disconcerting to a rider used to flex. I imagine that type of skip-slide is also slower for racing, and less safe overall.

Very "flexy" boards, on the other hand, can present their own problems. As you go over a bump, the board will flex down, cushioning the impact, but it will also spring back up. If you are turning at the top of the rebound, little weight will be on the wheels and the board will want to slide. Again, this is less safe.

The right amount of flex will keep the wheels on the ground and make the ride more controllable. It might also make a luge faster on a twisty road.

Stand-up Skateboarders can use flex to "pump" their boards side to side and generate forward momentum. As they turn, some of the energy goes into flexing the board against the sideways grip of the wheels. This energy is returned to the rider as the board straightens back up. If the board is still turning, there is no effect on forward momentum; it's just bouncing. However, if the energy is returned at the moment the wheels are straightened up, the result is a little jolt of acceleration.

You can measure the flex of your luge by placing modeling clay under the lowest part between the front and rear wheels. Set the empty board onto the clay so it slightly smashes. This will give you a way to measure the clearance of an empty board. Next, kneel on the board and bounce up and down. The clay will smash and hold the minimum ground clearance, which you can now measure when you get off the board.

The amount of flex will also determine how low your luge can sit. A board with an inch of flex shouldn't be designed to sit 1/2" off the ground.

If after some time, your luge seems to have more flex than when it was new, you need to do a thorough inspection. Additional flex may indicate delaminating wood or fiberglass; or for a metal board, a broken weld or metal fatigue. Additionally, aluminum boards develop less flex over time as the metal "work hardens." By taking a baseline measurement when your board is new, you can give it periodic "health checkups."

Non-Measured Characteristics

There are other qualities which are important to your board, but which are not readily measured. Among these are durability, repairability, and transportability. Design ultimately determines performance in these areas, but materials play a big part as well. If a true debate takes place over the advantages of wood, metal, and composites; the arguments would have to focus on these areas.

Durability

Having your board hauled up the hill after every run is the biggest test of its durability. Other riders dump their sharp metal edges onto the middle of your board. If you have an expensive paint job, kiss it good-bye.

Tipping your board over at speed will also test its durability. Grind a side against the pavement at 30 mph and find out what an effective belt sander the road is.

On my racing wood board, I've attached steel skid plates to the edges where the board will scrape when tipped on its side. Wood or fiberglass scrape away more quickly than metal, so I'd have to say that a metal board will be more durable in the long run.

Repairability

One of the main reasons to build a wood board is that it is quick and inexpensive to make. The same quality also makes it easy to repair. Wood putty or Bondo™ lets you fill in the ground away or gouged bits. If you spray paint your board you can make quick repairs overnight. By the same token, however, a metal board is more durable, and therefore less likely to need repair. If you lack repair skills, you'll be better off buying a prefabricated metal luge.

The inherent flexibility of wood or composites means you are not going to bend the chassis of a wood board. If you bend the chassis on a metal board it's usually unrepairable. Metal advocates claim wood boards are a hazard because they splinter when you crash them. The truth is, there are piles of metal boards with broken welds or bent chassis out there, but I've seen only one racing wood board break. It was a flimsy reject that had been beefed up with metal supports and broke at the joints when it was crashed on purpose. Had the board been any good to begin with, I'm sure it could have been put back together. But that doesn't mean you can't build your own crappy wood board that's a hazard to yourself and others.

If you are planning on building your own luge or buying it from someone else, make sure you have the ability to repair the damage from minor incidents yourself or are armed with a stock of spare parts.

Transportability

If you are a recreational rider, transportable means what you can fit into your trunk or on a roof rack. If you want to be a street luge racer, consider how easy your board will be to get onto a plane.

Michael Shannon (founder of RAIL East) travels with his fixed rail a lot and says you'll do OK by putting on junk wheels and letting the airline deal with it.

When I had a metal board built for the X Games, I made sure the pieces in front of and behind the wheels bolted on. Then I had a surf board company make a custom bag for the largest section. It has a shoulder strap and fits in my back seat. When I show up at a race and unzip my transportable luge bag, I'm hoping it gives the impression of the pool shark that has his own breakdown stick.

Similarly, my teammate Dave Auld built a 2"x4" and plywood board that bolted together. He wasn't trying to impress anyone, he just had to get the board between New Jersey and California for an event once a month. The wood holes were sloppy so it never seemed to bolt together straight. Guys hated that when he kicked their butts in a race.

Acceptability

This is the trickiest part of being creative with your board design. If for some reason the people with whom you want to ride don't accept your board, you won't get invited.

Actually, recreational riders are very accepting of diversity, because they are hoping to learn something new from you. It's when you start dealing with racing organizations and *rules* that things get tricky.

I've raced wooden boards in FIGR, EDI, and IGSA races. When I raced RAIL and RAIL East, I had to ride a metal board. Someday maybe RAIL will have a standard which accepts well-built wooden boards. Or perhaps EDI will make new rules against them.

I wish I could tell you that if you build a safe and functional board, that you will be able to race it anywhere. The truth is, before you plan to race in any organization, see what their members accept as legitimate competition equipment (it can go way beyond material types). You can then build a board to meet their specifications. Or race with an organization more suited to your needs.

Ultimately, it's your butt on the line and you shouldn't be forced to use equipment you don't believe in. By the same token, the promoter is responsible for what happens at their event. Respect the rules they feel are necessary for a safe race.

Kits and Design Plans

One of the biggest requests on the Internet is "Please tell me how to build a street luge." This book is the natural outcome of that request. In fact, it started as a series of e-mails to Zac Bernstein, who read about the sport and later became an accomplished racer.

I haven't been big on supplying blue prints for a luge, mostly because I believe they need to be custom fit. I've already discussed what I believe to be the critical dimensions, and how to fit them to your body. No doubt, some people will still want a set of measured plans.

I'm sure there will be a future business for people selling plans to build a competitive street luge. There seems to be a demand, and given the product liability aspects, it makes sense to sell plans or kits instead of the actual thing. There are probably markets for all three.

In the following pages, I include four basic drawings, three of which I've raced. I'm including the metal design used by my teammate Dave Auld because it is very typical. Dave also races wood and wanted to show that he could be fast on a very basic metal design. (He is.)

Two of these boards are reasonably straight forward to build (particularly the Classic design). I didn't include other drawings because I didn't want to give away anybody else's design that they might feel is proprietary. If you don't have the skills to design your own luge without a detailed blueprint then you should consider buying a kit or prefabricated board.

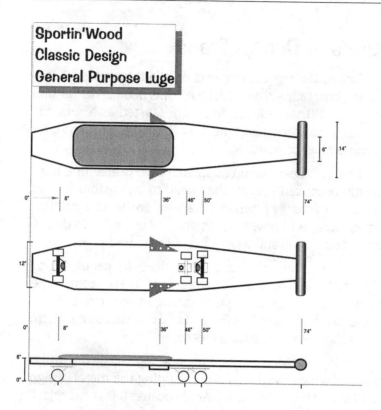

Sportin'Wood
Classic Design
General Purpose Luge

This is another view of my Classic Wood Board. It's unbelievably easy to make with basic hardware store materials. After scaling it to your size, cut the body out of high quality 3/4" plywood. Power tools are great, but you can even use a hand saw. Make sure you file and sand all the edges until they're smooth. You can fill and paint the wood to make a splinter-free surface. I needed to finish the board on the back cover in one night so I put black cloth tape all around the edges (after sanding). Then I used floor vinyl for the top and bottom. Stick it on, flip it over, cut to size. It's resistant to scuffs and cleans up with Mop-n-Glo™!

The pegs are fashioned from a section of 3/4" aluminum angle. It fits right over the nose. Orient it so the metal is touching the front and bottom edges of the board. Drill three holes and use the same type screws and nuts you'll use to attach your trucks. Never use nails. I've tried wooden pegs, but they seem to break off too easily and are harder to attach. The aluminum angle is light and bends when you hit something. You won't be able to bend it back, but you can still ride with a bent peg. Pipe insulation is a pre-slit foam tube. Slide it over the pegs and duct tape it.

The seat can be made from practically anything or even omitted. A carpet remnant is cheap and comfortable. You can stick it down with thick double backed tape, or place short wood screws down from the top corners.

Handles are the tricky part. My first board had the triangles screwed flush to the sides. It was difficult to do and they weren't very strong. I attached the handles underneath on my newer version of this style. They stay on great and I like my body position with my hands down low. But because they are low and unprotected, I've smacked my knuckles against lane reflectors and road debris. Think about how handles would work mounted on the top instead. Or get really good gloves.

I've found beginners feel comfortable on this board. Some drop designs don't feel as natural and this is an easy board to maneuver. Because it is short and has excellent ground clearance, it will ride on all sorts of roads that dropped boards can't make.

I've successfully raced this board against the highest tech boards out there. On twisty roads under 50 mph, where rider skill is paramount, it works well. If your friends with fancy aluminum rails make fun of you, tell them, "It's RETRO, baby!"

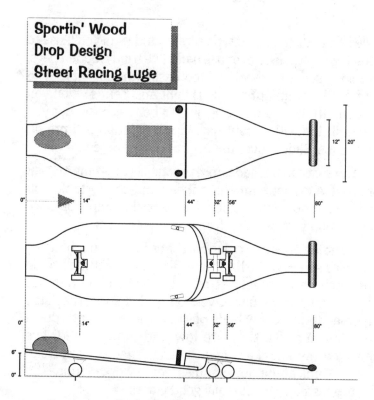

Sportin' Wood
Drop Design
Street Racing Luge

Some guys feel wood is "low tech" or "hokey." Imagine their dismay when they are beaten by this extra wide, all wood luge. It even has a coffee table oak finish. And in '96 and '97 it set the fastest pro qualifying time at 3 races. Bad boy Tom Mason put it best when he exclaimed, "I can't believe it, I was beat by a TREE!"

I liked wood for this design as it was easy to sand and shape the drop to be more aerodynamic. Be careful building drop boards out of wood though. Plywood is very strong in all directions, except when it is pulled apart at the drop. Don't be tempted to make sections too narrow, or beef them up with metal supports. Use high grade plywood that doesn't have voids.

Our team has successfully raced several boards of this design. All in all, it's fast and highly unique.

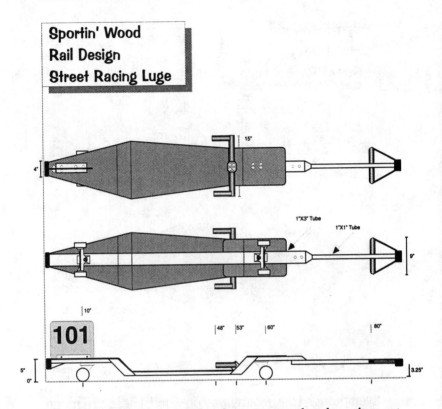

Sportin' Wood Rail Design Street Racing Luge

Dave Auld is one of the few racers who doesn't want anything to do with building or prepping boards. He just wants to go fast and then get a ride back up the hill. When faced with the task of designing a custom metal luge he wanted the path of least resistance (and cost).

He selected the basic Bullet Board steel tube chassis, and requested a Moe Speed type front end. He shortened the standard wheelbase to 50" and went with a Marcus Rietema style seat and handlebars.

The nose is dropped to meet bumper specs and to help with an aerodynamic body position. The steel chassis is gusseted and welded. The pan and fenders are made from a surplus road sign. Plastic car trim is self adhesive and covers the sharp edges of the pan.

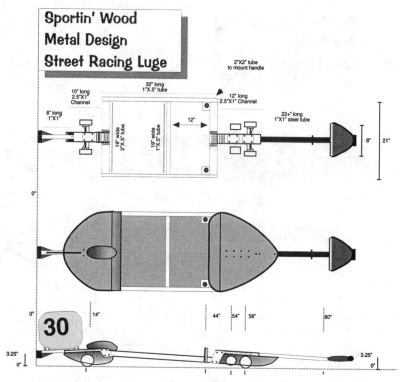

Sportin' Wood Metal Design Street Racing Luge

Even though I earned my way on wood, I needed a metal board to compete in the '97 X Games. Fortunately, Dean Salter and Jim Kiper of Bullet Board custom built a steel luge to my specifications. I was really worried that switching to a metal design at the last minute would hinder my performance, but this board set the fastest speed in competition. That I took a Bronze medal in the dual luge, while Biker Sherlock ran away with 2 Golds and a Silver(!) is attributable to the racers, then, and not just their equipment.

I found building my first metal board to be a pain. You have to really watch the weight, and you can't just sand shapes to be aerodynamic. I'm glad Jim is a certified welder, and caution anyone playing around with welding their own board, especially if it's aluminum. If a weld breaks, you usually have a catastrophic failure.

Dean and Jim learned that lesson early when they saw a friend of theirs go over a bump and his home welded luge snapped in half. He slid under a parked truck and had to go to the hospital with a broken arm. Consequently, Jim takes luge welds very seriously. Make sure your welder does too.

A really nice feature that came from building the metal board is that I designed the major components to bolt together. When I travel, the board can be disassembled into a 36" package. I can also carry extra front and rear sections in case something gets bent in a crash.

To get back at the guys who didn't want to get beat by a "hokey" wood board, I covered the top surfaces with Rubbermaid™ Wood Grained shelf paper! The shape is wide and ship-like so one of the kids watching the X Games dubbed it "The Pirate Ship."

I haven't included these board designs because mine are cooler and everyone should build them like I do. One of the best parts of the sport is all of the great ideas that come to every race in the form of original street luge boards. Half of the current participants have at least as much fun designing new equipment as actually riding it.

The ultimate street luge has not been invented, but a lot of guys keep trying. Having a single "clone" spec which everyone has to ride would kill the fun for most racers. It would also kill the improvements that make our boards faster and safer. If it were not for evolution, we'd still be riding 3 foot skate boards on our butts.

Celebrate the diversity!

Wheels, Trucks, Bearings

Mounted under the luge is the part that ties our sport to skateboarding. Even as we develop trucks and wheels specifically for street luge, they will only be bigger, stronger, and hopefully safer versions of what our stand-up brethren use.

Using a lean-turn skateboard system is one of the most enjoyable parts of the sport. Leaning into a turn is what makes motorcycles and skis so much fun. A skateboard system is also extremely simple and therefore affordable. You can literally take the trucks off a drug store skateboard and bolt them to a long piece of plywood—presto, cheap luge! Of course it will be slow and handle poorly. If you go on too steep a grade you will crash and get hurt. But hey, you could have done that on the cheap skateboard. And since you're laying down and wearing protective gear (right?), you're *already* working on keeping injuries to a minimum.

Some racers will be aghast that I would even suggest a crappy luge would work. To them it's instant death. First of all, a crappy luge will work whether I mention it or not. And people *will* figure it out. They have been for over twenty years without any help from me.

If you have crappy equipment and poor judgement, you will crash often. If you have excellent equipment and use the same poor judgement, you will crash at higher speeds. I'll help out with equipment suggestions, but our worst accidents happen because of poor decisions, not poor equipment.

Wheels

I've seen really neat boards perform poorly because of wheel choice. Wheels make a dramatic difference in the handling, reliability, speed, and safety of your board. Not a subtle difference—a dramatic difference.

First we can start by eliminating obvious poor choices. I was corresponding with one aspiring rider who complained of constant instability and crashes. We wrote of wheel manufacture, durometer, and size. It wasn't until he asked why the guys at the ESPN Extreme Games were riding the "old, wide skateboard wheels" that I realized he was working with in-line skate wheels! For God's sake, don't make the mistake of running in-line wheels just because they are readily available. This sport is overly abusive on wide, tall skateboard wheels, which already wear out quickly, delaminate, or melt down. Go to a tall, thin in-line wheel and you will quickly find out the value of leathers and a helmet.

Plus, my own experiments (conducted by a professional rider under controlled conditions, of course) showed in-line wheels to be slower for luge, even though they were taller and narrower. I expected to pick up a lot of speed because of reduced rolling resistance, but what happened was I lost speed scrubbing through even the most gradual turns. On a 45 mph hill, I lost 3 mph.

Another loser option is the ubiquitous "mini-wheel" used by most skateboarders today. I suppose they may be good for "tricks," but Real Men prefer big block engines, voluptuous women, and large, wide street luge wheels. Every time I go into a new skate shop only to find little rock wheels, I feel like my father on a "These kids today . . . !" tirade. Perhaps the increasing popularity of long board skateboarding will put wheels back into the skate shops that we can use for luge.

The wheels you want are tall (usually measured in millimeters), wide, and soft (measured in durometer). It used to be that the favored street luge wheel was the 70 mm red Kryptonics™. Although they had a reputation for melting down during long, fast runs, they were speedy and held in the turns. Kryptonics still makes them but supposedly won't sell them for street luge because some bonehead sued them after crashing. Now they are marketed for classic roller skates and are consequently more hard to find. Kryps have regained popularity among racers although the company is emphatic that their wheels are not rated for over 30 mph and are definitely "not suited for Street Luge Road Racing." (Although a few racers have had some sort of sponsorship deal with them??)

The truth be known, no wheels exist as of this writing that are truly designed for the stresses we put on them. If you plan to sue when you crash just because your wheels came apart, please find something else to do.

Hyper™ makes another current favorite in street luge wheels. The Super Mundo™ is 72 mm tall and is adequately soft. Mundos don't seem to melt as easily as the Kryps, but they do "chunk" apart when ridden hard. Special bonded versions are available for a couple of bucks more, and are supposed to help hold the urethane to the plastic inner rim better. They seem to chunk apart also, so I buy them 16 at a time and just replace them more frequently.

There are fans of other wheel brands, including Gravity™ Super-G Wheels, Road Warriors™, and especially Labeda™. My team has raced with Labeda 90 mm wheels for over two years and we're really pleased with the performance. To date, I would have to say that the Labeda 90 mm wheels are the best street luge wheels available. Why? They use aluminum hubs and excellent urethane. They combine the best in grippiness, precision, and wear

Wheel Diameter	Spin	Speed
60 mm	10,000 rpm	70 mph
70 mm	10,000 rpm	82 mph
80 mm	10,000 rpm	94 mph
90 mm	10,000 rpm	105 mph
100 mm	10,000 rpm	117 mph
127 mm	10,000 rpm	148 mph

of any wheel I have seen or tried. Additionally, I believe we benefit from their larger diameter.

To try to get a handle on how wheel size could improve speed, I assumed a limiting spin of 10,000 rpm. Of course, bearing rotation isn't the sole factor determining top speed, but it contributes.

As you can see from the table, larger diameter wheels can make a big difference. Aside from rotating more slowly at the same speed, larger wheels will also roll more easily over cracks and other imperfections. They have more surface area touching the ground and should therefore grip in the turns better. The only downside for racing is that larger diameter wheels seem to accelerate more slowly than smaller ones.

Some new riders worry that large wheels will carry them to dangerous speeds and so they would be safer sticking to smaller wheels. In practice, however, guys with 70 mm wheels seem to be going *just about as fast* as guys with 90mm wheels. Other factors apparently determine a rider's speed much more than just wheel diameter. So if a hill and the rider can support 80 mph, the wheels will come along as well. Unless they blow up.

The big difference in wheel diameter is that at 82 mph, 90 mm wheels are spinning at 7,800 rpm while the 70 mm wheels are pulling slightly over 10,000 rpm. If there is a magic rpm at which wheels come apart, equivalent 90 mm wheels will be at only 78% of their failure speed when the smaller wheels explode.

Rick Wilson of XTreme Wheelz™ (the off-road skateboard wheel company) has been studying street luge and says he is committed to producing the best, fastest, safest luge wheels ever. He hasn't made the fastest wheels yet but I would definitely keep an eye on his stuff. The experience gained in making bomb proof off-road wheels certainly comes in handy in designing durable luge wheels. And if you are just starting out, larger, slower, more durable wheels may be just what you need when learning the sport.

A few other manufacturers have also been toying with street luge wheels, not to mention new wheel designs by companies already in the top spots. So by the time you read this, there may be a new king of the hill.

Historically, racing rules have allowed maximum luge wheel diameters between 70 mm and 5 inches (127 mm). Personally, I favor whatever promotes safe, affordable, long lasting performance from our wheels.

Trucks

Since the focus of this book is supposed to be street luge survival, I'll drop back to some basics that can injure you if you mess up.

As with other skateboards, trucks are mounted to your board in opposite directions. The front trucks have the front pivot facing forward. The back trucks have the pivot facing backward. When you lean left, the front left wheel should come back toward you and the rear left wheel should move forward toward you. That is, **the front and back trucks steer in opposite directions**.

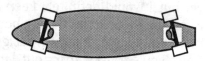

Now while this seems blatantly obvious to most skateboarders, the potential for having one or both trucks mounted backward is greater as you start swapping trucks when tuning your street luge. It's hot, your friends are yelling "C'mon, let's luge!" The trucks are far enough apart that you don't see the mistake as it happens. In fact, almost every rider I know (including me) has gotten into a rush and mounted a truck backward. You lean left; it goes right, and you think "What the hell?" Fortunately, I caught my error when trying to ride my board from the garage to the car. My teammate John Cazin complained of poor handling after a squirrelly qualifying run. The problem? A backward truck. How he ever got all the way down the course without crashing is still beyond me. A woman had an horrendous crash at the Signal Hill races when she attempted the hill with a truck mounted backward.

If you already know about trucks from skateboarding, your biggest question is probably "What kind should I buy for street luge?" Until the mid '80s the type of trucks you used wasn't really a critical factor in high performance.

Bob Pereyra (founder of RAIL) told me he was sorting through a box of odd skateboard trucks one day and came across Z-Rollers™. Today, most professional racers use them. They are considerably more expensive than standard trucks and make changing wheels a pain.

I bought a set a few years ago and have been hooked ever since. Z's are distinguished by having an axle that is covered by a vinyl coated roller and the whole unit spins on two extra bearings. The downside is that the wheels are much more difficult to take on and off because you have to lock down both sides of the axle to remove a nut. Half the time, the wrong side comes off and all your bearings and washers dump into the dirt. The axles seem to get bent all the time and are expensive and time consuming to replace.

Along comes Moe Speed Axles™ to the rescue! Moe is a racer that was tired of the finicky rollers. He designs and manufactures an axle/roller replacement that's *much* easier to work with and cuts down on bent axles. I consider them a necessity for a Z-Roller racing set up. And they drive the price up even further.

Some people don't believe Z-Rollers are a necessary expense. Professional racer Lee Dansie continues to turn out top finishes on extra wide Independent™ trucks. No spinning axles, high availability, low cost. If Lee can win on inexpensive trucks, you can certainly have a good time riding them. Pick wide trucks that are a brand name, or look closely at the construction. I once bought a set of cheap trucks that snapped off when my wheel clipped a tire barrier.

I think the next breakthrough in street luge may come through a better truck design. Hopefully by the time you read this book, it will have already occurred, but designs have remained pretty stable for the past 20 years.

If you design a system that doesn't use "lean-turn" as the method of steering, then you are moving out of Street Luge and into Gravity Cars. I've seen some slick designs that have independent suspension, anti-lock brakes, and push-pull steering, but they couldn't race in the luge class. They also weren't faster, but a lot of different variables come into play. Needless to say, "lean-turn" is a defining characteristic of street luge and all designs begin there.

The main problem with skateboard trucks is that they were designed for sharp turns at slow speeds with a short wheelbase. The reason most people are terrified of street luge is because of "speed wobbles." If you ride a standard skateboard fast enough, i.e. over 30 mph, you will encounter this dreaded phenomenon. In essence, speed wobbles are a rapid back and forth oscillation against your will, which could rapidly throw you off the board at high speed. Nobody likes speed wobbles. They make you crash.

There are at least four ways to reduce speed wobbles on a luge. First is to increase the wheel base. The further apart the trucks, the less they seem to want to turn rapidly and thus shake you off your mount. Stand-up downhill skateboards are extra long versions of regular skateboards for this very reason. Street luge boards have even longer wheelbases, but remember that the longer the wheelbase, the wider the turning radius.

Another option is to tighten the trucks. This means clamping down the urethane cushions (also called "rubbers" or "bushings") so that more force is needed to initiate a turn. Once you have a set wheelbase, this is your most likely option, and you will tighten or loosen your trucks according to the course you ride. A similar option is to replace the cushions with those of a stiffer compound. Both of these options have one major drawback. As you stiffen the trucks to prevent speed wobbles, you will find that they no longer lean easily enough to leave all your wheels on the ground in hard turns. The outside wheels angle up into the air, instead of pivoting forward as designed. Consequently, the amount of urethane against the road in a hard turn is effectively halved, and you will slide, scrubbing off speed, unless you spin-out or crash.

A wider wheelbase for extra leverage or leverage from your board can force tight trucks to lean, thus keeping all wheels on the road.

The historical racing width limit for trucks has been set at 12". I assumed this was artificially narrow and had special aftermarket parts made to extend my trucks to the 12" max. Aside from being plagued with bent axles, the extra width introduced another unexpected result. The trucks *were* more stable. However, I noticed a strange steering lag which I was initially unable to identify. I think this is the explanation:

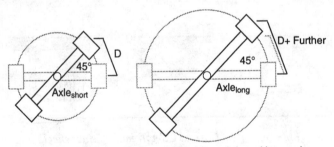

Further = $\pi(\text{Axle}_{long} - \text{Axle}_{short})(\text{angle}/360)$

With skateboard lean steering, the wheels are fixed to the axle and the whole axle pivots. That means the wheels have to travel forward or back in order to turn. The longer the axle is, the further the wheels must travel in order to affect the same steering angle. With skateboard trucks, a wider wheelbase means slower steering response. Cars don't have this problem because turning the wheels is independent of the width of the track width (the distance between the center of the left and right wheels).

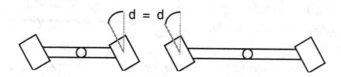

Another very effective option to reduce speed wobbles (which can be used in conjunction with all other options) is to modify the angle of your trucks.

There is an inverse relationship between how hard it is to initiate a turn and how far the wheels can pivot forward or back. That means you can angle the truck to be easier to lean, but it won't turn much, or angle it to turn a lot, but it will be hard to lean.

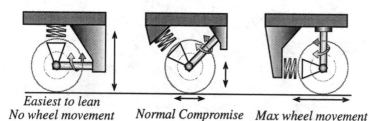

Easiest to lean
No wheel movement   *Normal Compromise*   *Max wheel movement*
But impossible to lean

If experienced riders modify the angle of their trucks, it is usually to angle the back of the rear truck downward. This renders it easier to lean the back trucks (which have less weight over them) with less forward and backward

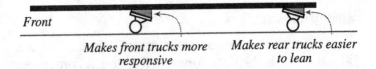

Front

Makes front trucks more responsive   *Makes rear trucks easier to lean*

wheel motion (which helps reduce speed wobbles). Conversely, more turn per lean angle in the front trucks is desirable, so most riders leave the front base plate flat relative to the road. Depending on the built-in angle of the trucks, some riders will even put wedge pads in front, angling the back of the front trucks forward, increasing turn sensitivity.

Not leaving well enough alone, I kept increasing the front angle until I ended up with a board that turned sharply and went very fast without speed wobbles. Unfortunately, when you took your feet off the front end (usually to brake) the whole board became unstable and spit you off. Experiment with new steering geometries cautiously, and at slower speeds.

The fourth and best way to deal with the problem is to use trucks that were designed to have less desire to oscillate in the first place. Dan Gesmer's Seismic™ trucks were designed with special opposed rebound springs to help return energy and a geometry to reduce oscillations. They haven't been optimized for street luge yet, but eliminating the traditional urethane cushions is a step in the right direction.

Currently, only Randal™ is trying to optimize trucks for this sport, with wide floating axles and modified pivot angles. Randal (the actual guy) comes to a lot of races and continually incorporates feedback into his next design. Consequently, more and more racers are switching to Randal Speed Trucks™, citing benefits of a tunable system that was purpose built for luge.

Extra Traction

Another separation between street luge and regular skateboarding is the need for extra traction. As previously mentioned, cornering ability ultimately limits your top speed on a twisty road.

Since it's most critical to maintain traction in front, it's where most riders concentrate. In the following discussions, I'll be referring to front and back sets of wheels as they are mounted to the front of the luge. Depending on how your board handles, you may consider beefing up the traction at the rear of your luge as well.

Adding a **second set** of trucks right behind the first will double the amount of contact with the ground and give you better traction. It also distributes the load. Heavy riders

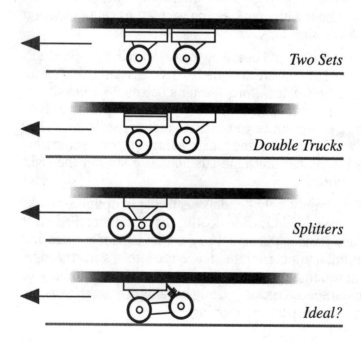

Two Sets

Double Trucks

Splitters

Ideal?

may need to do this just to prevent overtaxing their wheels. Make sure the two sets of trucks both point the same direction. As the second truck introduces a slightly different turning arc, mount it as close to the first truck as possible. You can minimize the different arcs by using the same brand of trucks and wheels.

When I first learned to ride, Dave Perry showed me the trick of **Double Trucks**. In this case, another truck is mounted just behind the first one, but with the wheels slightly off the ground. You can achieve this by using a thick pad on one truck and a thin pad on the other. The idea here is that the second set of wheels don't drag on the ground when you are going straight, but when you lean into a turn they touch and provide extra traction. It works great!

The only weakness with double trucks is that only the inside wheel of the raised set will touch the ground. The other extra wheel stays in the air. Also, the turning arc of the secondary set is not the same as the primary set. This is because the arc is initiated by lean contact, which the secondary set starts later. I try to compensate for this by actually using different trucks and wheels for the secondary set.

The big problem seems to be getting a secondary set of wheels on the ground while keeping the same turning angle. I saw a picture of trucks someone custom made in the '70s that had double axles. Of course! Since they share a common pivot, two axles on the same truck ensures the wheels stay at the same angle. The only problem is in making the custom trucks.

Some racers recently got the brilliant idea to mount a small pivot bar to each side of their existing trucks which has the same advantages. They call them **Splitters.** Moe Speed™ Street Luge Equipment now sells splitters for Z-Rollers under the name **Moe-Traction**™.

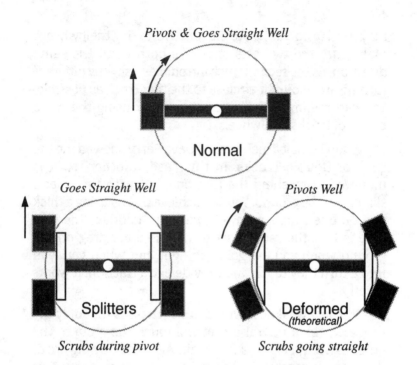

Splitters are two aluminum bars with a hole drilled in the middle and pivot independently on either side of the axle. They each have two short axle sections on which to mount the four wheels (see diagram). Moe has even started drilling the middle hole off-center, so you can flip the splitters over for more or less ground clearance. Pretty innovative.

In an experiment, Moe made a special extra long set so I could try 90 mm wheels with the Splitters. Surprisingly, I had to fight to initiate the turns, which really destabilized and slowed the board. In gradual corners they were fine. I believe the problem stems from having the contact patches of the front and back wheels too far apart. They don't fight in the turns like two separate sets of trucks would. Instead, they fight to prevent turns. "To minimize the problem", says Jarret "Dr. Go Fast" Ewanek, "you should reduce the 'Scrub Zone' by keeping the center of the wheels closer together."

Theoretically, you could completely fix the turning problem by making deformed wide splitters with the wheels pre-angled along the turning circumference. They would turn easily but wouldn't go in a straight line, so don't expect Moe to be making any.

My **ideal** solution to the problem is a design that combines the lower drag and easy turning of double trucks, with the single pivot benefits of a Splitter. This design keeps the back wheels off the ground when going straight and has a linkage which forces **both secondary wheels** to bite down in the turns. Furthermore, because they are connected to the same pivot, they will maintain the same turning arc as the front two. Because they are not touching the ground at the beginning of the turn, the trucks will pivot as nimbly as a single set. (As no one makes trucks like these yet my whole theory is still untested.)

As a racer, the main concern about four front wheels is the extra drag. However, in the 1997 X Games, the number 1 and 2 fastest qualifiers were running Splitters. The in-line skate racers at the games were not surprised. Competitor Scott Peer revealed that in-line racers depend on using more wheels to better distribute the load and keep them fast.

Of course the **simplest option** of all is to use wheels that provide you with enough traction from a single set. After years of running double trucks, this year's racing board is tuned for a single set of 90 mm wheels in front, and it seems to handle more predictably and hold a better turn than my previous boards.

Regardless of the speed or even handling advantages there is a good reason to have a second set of trucks and wheels: **Redundancy**. On several occasions when I have had a catastrophic wheel failure ("puked a wheel") I was able to maintain control over the board because it dropped back onto its second front set.

Bearings

When I first started riding, bearings were designated by brand or country of origin. Debates raged whether "Swiss" or "German" bearings were better. It was like choosing from a wine list in a foreign restaurant.

ABEC

Fortunately, the Annular Bearing Engineering Council (ABEC) created a precision rating scale for the type of bearings we use. You normally see ABEC rated bearings in odd increments: 1,3,5,7,9. The higher the ABEC rating, the higher the precision fit of the parts. ABEC 1s come standard in most toy store type wheels. You'll want to run at least ABEC 3s.

ABEC 5s are still at a slight premium (although coming down rapidly in price) so most racers play on 3s and race new 5s. I haven't done any scientific correlations on street luge top speeds and ABEC ratings. I do however notice improvement from 1s to 3s and ABEC 5s perform even better. But I have also heard that some companies put shields stamped ABEC 5 onto bearings that were not originally manufactured to that tolerance level.

There is also a line of thought that tighter tolerances don't make the bearings any faster. I've had friends that spent big money on special ABEC 9s that seemed slower than their ABEC 5s. ABEC isn't a speed rating.

In fact, some of my bearings that spin the longest unloaded are "Swiss" bearings that have no ABEC rating on them at all. But that doesn't discount precision bearings.

While a bearing with a higher ABEC rating may not be faster, don't confuse tight tolerances with tight bearings. Tolerance refers to how closely the parts measure to a specification, not necessarily how tightly they fit. Precision fit is one of the components determining bearing performance. So, I've come to count on ABEC 5 bearings when picking out what to prepare for a race.

Because there are still so few street lugers, manufacturers are not motivated to make improved equipment just for us. We have in-line skaters to thank for the availability of ABEC 5s and bearings rated ABEC 7 are starting to show up for the recreational market. Until we grow as a sport, look to piggyback on in-line skating improvements

I actually ordered a bearing distributor's catalog looking for formulas to pick better bearings. There is a rated life calculation which seems fairly impressive. This is the upshot: The more load you place on bearings, the shorter they will last; the higher speed you run bearings, the shorter they will last. Between the two destructive influences, heavier is worse than faster. Terminator™ Bearings indicates its ABEC 3s are rated for **700 lbs at 70 mph.** A quick follow up call confirmed that was **per bearing!**

So as long as they're maintained, bearings may help determine who rolls faster or slower, but they aren't the weak link for this sport.

Ceramics

Ceramic bearings made a big splash at the '97 X Games when Chris Ponsetti and Dennis Derammelaere qualified #1 and #2 respectively. They credited their performance to Ninja Ceramix™ bearings.

I also used ceramic-based bearings which I purchased through an ad found in an in-line skating magazine. They cost close to $200 for eight so you can imagine my horror when they showed up looking exactly like any other bearings! It turns out, that only the balls are ceramic. The rest of the bearing is conventional. I would have called foul, except these bearings spun like no other. When fitted in wheels, good bearings spin about 2 minutes; my race ready ABEC 5s spin for about 4 minutes; and these ceramics spun for 8 minutes!

I managed to qualify #3 behind Chris and Dennis, so I definitely think there is a correlation between ceramic bearings and high performance. However, I have had the top qualifying time when racing without ceramic bearings, and so have Chris and Dennis.

There is no way I would dump that kind of money into bearings if I were not racing. And after a few days of racing, the ceramics didn't spin any better than my standard racing bearings, including when I set the fastest speed on the course.

So, yes, I think high tech bearings can make a difference in races where 1/100 of a second is critical. But you can win races without spending the extra money, and you can certainly have a great time riding with inexpensive bearings.

Shields

Exposed to road grime, ball bearings rapidly load with grit, slowing the wheels and shortening bearing life. This is why most bearings come with shields. Even with shields, though, grit will find its way into your bearings. So you can clean them or throw them away.

Removable shields allow efficacious cleansing of your bearings. Keep a safety pin in your tool kit. It seems to be the only tool which can quickly help you get the shields off, particularly if the outside of the bearing is dirty. Some premium bearings already come with one shield removed. This allows you to rapidly clean the bearings when they are out of the wheel and if you turn the shield side out, they shouldn't get dirty any faster.

Lubrication

I haven't had "Factory Training" in bearing cleansing, but the hot fix seems to be soaking them in lacquer thinner and then blowing them dry with compressed air. Some people prefer carburetor cleaner as it both dissolves grease and sprays away the grime. Other people claim compressed air can ruin unloaded bearings or force the dirt into cracks. If this were the type of book to be filled with legal disclaimers, I'd make a big case about the care required in dealing with volatile fluids like lacquer thinner. However, since your big worry right now is not going under the wheels of an oncoming car, I'll limit my advice:

This is the "Street Luge Survival Guide." Not "Surviving Your Dad's Garage." The tools I talk about can easily cut off your fingers and volatile liquids can blind you and burn down your house. If you can't name three ways the stuff I mention can maim you, keep asking until you find someone who can.

OK, back to street luge.

So your bearings are squeaky clean. (Actually, if they squeak, throw them out.) And they really spin like crazy. **DON'T FORGET to lubricate them!** Your bearings will rust or worse yet, seize, melt your wheels, and toss you into a curb at high speed.

Most racers soak out the grease that comes standard with bearings and replace it with a thin oil for fast starts. Just like with an engine, though, you should worry that the thin oil will burn off, resulting in inadequate lubrication. If you don't require maximum performance over short distances, remember that the grease was initially put in your bearings for a reason.

Alignment

Wheels with imperfect hubs will allow bearings within a wheel to cock and fight each other. And that would be slower, wouldn't it?

In-line skaters use thinner axles and a precision spacer which holds the bearings parallel. They claim it makes even more difference than 2 steps up the ABEC scale. With all of the regular axles I've bent, I'd recommend paying a premium for precision hubs instead.

And while we're on the subject of misaligned bearings, bent axles cause whole wheels to fight each other and misaligned trucks can be even worse. If you're looking for performance, pay close attention that **everything lines up straight.**

Side Loads

So here we are at the last part of the most tedious section of the book. I've purposely left out any entertaining graphics, and even resorted to words like "efficacious" to throw off the less-deserving. The use of bold letters on "Don't forget to lubricate them" and "...everything lines up straight" should cause experienced racers to sigh and dismiss this whole section as for beginners only. Good.

I wanted at least one good secret for the book, and hey, it may not even really work.

It all started with the free floating axles in Z-Roller trucks. Z-Rollers were intended for skateboarders to grind along curbs smoothly without damaging anything. Supposedly, that took the fun out of grinding. But a great side benefit is that for street luge, most racers feel Z-Rollers are noticeably faster than trucks without spinning axles.

I tried to get my dad to machine heavier rollers, citing a "momentum theory" of performance. I reasoned that the fast spinning roller was acting as a flywheel, building up momentum and driving the wheels longer. My theory met with great reluctance. Dad cited his "you have your head up your butt" theory, and countered my "you've never ridden Z-Rollers" with his "you've never worked in aerospace." Eventually he convinced me that energy was not being transferred back into forward momentum.

Skate bearings were designed primarily for straight up and down loads. Street luge, on the other hand, introduces terrific side loads. When the side loads meet skate bearings, the result is bearings binding against the axle.

Floating axles begin spinning when a bearing binds against them, thereby (ah ha!) reducing drag. In this way, the wheels spin more freely longer than with conventional trucks.

The real answer, of course, is to prevent binding in the first place; either through redesigned wheels, bearings, and axles; or through the addition of thrust bearings (notice no bold, capitals, or graphics).

These bearings are thin like washers and usually come in three pieces: a center piece with exposed roller bearings and two very smooth outer washers. Putting a set on the left and right of the wheel transfers the side loads into the thrust bearing before the regular bearing has time to bind against the axle. That's the theory anyway.

On straightaways, you won't notice a difference, but as the course gets twistier you may appreciate the tip. If they aren't a standard part of every rider's arsenal by the time you read this, try Torrington bearing part numbers TRA512 and NTA512.

I do want to add, that the whole spinning axle craze is really based more on racing performance magic and less on actual engineering. The truth could be that a spinning axle doesn't contribute to better rolling performance at all. What makes them seem faster is that in order to spin, the axles must be perfectly straight. The minute an axle bends, the wheels start fighting each other and you slow down. The bend can be very slight, and with conventional trucks you'd never notice. A spinning axle, on the other hand, will no longer spin or will cause a back and forth gyration of one of the wheels. Because racers can immediately identify and replace a bent axle, their gear stays fast.

Gear

If you like to go fast, you're going to crash. And when you crash, gear is everything. Comfort and style can drive your decisions, but make sure you are adequately protected. A colorful Lycra speed suit might look neat and offer the least wind resistance, but it also offers the least asphalt resistance. Street luge without appropriate protection is like skydiving without a reserve chute, scuba diving without gauges, or rock climbing without ropes; it's plenty of fun until something goes wrong, and something always does. Plan for the fall when you go out to the edge.

There are actually a minority breed in every adventure sport which eschew protection. Every few years, they achieve notoriety because most people think adventure sports are crazy anyway. The argument inevitably sounds like, "If you're going to eat it, die like a man, not like some pansy in pads and a helmet."

I gotta love these guys. Basically, they suck at their sport and hope to compensate by upping the level of recklessness. They will issue challenges on their own terms, and feel vindicated when no one else accepts. Unfortunately, they never have enough time to attain proper skills or learn the truths of their sport, because in a few years they chicken out or end up on the disabled list. Face it. The fastest guys are going to crash a lot—pushing the edge. If they want to remain the fastest guys, they need to stay healthy. The "tough guys" end up drinking beer and yelling at the TV, or spending the rest of their lives with prosthetic devices.

Helmet

Motorcycle road racers have the same type of high speed asphalt wipe-outs that occur in street luge. In the absence of any specialized gear for our sport, we can take a lesson from them. Road racers wear full face helmets, and so should you. Don't risk grinding off your chin and lower jaw with an open face helmet. And if you've ever seen how quickly a bicycle helmet disintegrates, you wouldn't even consider one.

When choosing a full face helmet, there are a couple of aspects which differ from motorcycle usage. First, instead of looking upward inside the helmet as a road racer does, luge racers look down toward their chins. This is inherent in the riding positions of both sports. When you are trying on helmets, see how far over your head must be to look at your toes. You'll probably find this disqualifies a lot of helmets designed for motocross because of the large, rock-guard, type mouth protection. Second, many of the neat auto close and venting features designed for motorcycle use won't work from a luge position.

When this sport gets big, look for new aerodynamic and higher visibility designs. Bell™ and Sno-Rider™ have sold a Wedge™ helmet for snowmobile riders that's popular for luge. It has a low chin guard that sticks further forward than normal. Consequently, you can keep your head really low and still see. Racers replace the standard face shield with custom street luge ones that allow even better visibility. Since you don't look through the top part of the visor, you can plaster you name up there so your friends recognize you on TV.

For God's sake, please don't buy a helmet that is too large even though it allows you to position it for better visibility. When is a helmet too big?

TIGHTEN THE CHIN STRAP AND TRY TO PULL THE HELMET OFF FROM THE BACK OF THE HELMET. If you can pull it off, DON'T USE IT!

While I was still writing this book, my good friend Dave Perry (who taught me to luge) was killed when his helmet pulled off in a crash. He was trying to set the stand-up (Speedboarding) record so it wasn't a street luge accident, but it could have been. The helmet fit his face tightly, but even with a snug chin strap, it pulled off over his head. One second he was having the time of his life, and the next, his lifeless body was flopping along the pavement. I almost didn't finish this book because of it, but Dave would want you to ride with a safe helmet.

Gloves

This is where our gear needs to be even tougher than for road racing. Motorcycle gloves are designed in case your hands hit the ground at 60 mph. Street lugers pet the asphalt frequently, even when they don't crash.

Because you are so very low to the street, your hands need to be protected from continual asphalt contact, and most gloves wear through after just a few applications. Depending on your riding position and style, exactly how often your hands hit may vary. But if your hands are gripping down low and outside, they will be the first part of your body to hit in a hard sliding turn. Like a road racer's knee.

You may even put out a hand on the inside of a turn to help you slide around. Gloves don't like that, but your skin will like it less. It would be nice to encase your hands in some type of plastic armor, but you still need the dexterity to hold on to your board.

I haven't come across the perfect solution to hand protection but I'll offer four variations:

1. Get several pair of cheap but sturdy work gloves and just admit they are disposable items.

2. Figure out how not to touch the ground as much, ruining fewer gloves but missing an exciting part of the sport.

3. Get welder's gloves. What they lack in dexterity they make up for in toughness. They are ultimately less expensive than throwing away cheaper gloves and they provide better protection in a bad crash.

4. Get cool motorcycle gloves to match your leathers/luge outfit. They will have the best "feel" and aerodynamics. They will be so expensive that you won't have the heart

to throw them away after you quickly wear through them. You will resort to duct taping the holes and fingers thereby reducing the aero/dexterity advantage. Eventually you'll wind up gluing rubber or plastic bits to the worn areas, and look like some weird cyber-freak.

For racing, I've taken to wearing long rubber gloves over leather work gloves. They provide excellent grippiness for push starts and great aerodynamics. I only mention this on the rare chance that it becomes trendy and beginners don't realize the important layer of leather underneath. The latex may prevent "dishwater hands" but does nothing to prevent the "meat claws" you'd get without a more formidable barrier.

The most common disabling luge injury is to grind a knuckle to the bone, which will put you out of work until you heal. Worst case is you lose a finger. I have seen enough severe hand injuries in the sport to know we need technical improvement in this area still.

Street Luge Suit

Street Luge body protection usually evolves through four stages:

- Street clothes
- Jumpsuits
- Leathers
- Custom Leathers

Stage 1: Street Clothes

When beginning most sports, if you are typical, you'll try to "cheap-out." You figure you don't want to invest in a bunch of expensive specialized gear in case you'd really rather just watch it on TV.

Unless you already have leathers, you'll probably get out some of your old clothes to destroy. Never mind that the time when you need the most protection is when you are just starting. Denim pants will seem to offer the best protection of what you probably own. You'll grind right through them at anything over 25 mph so think about double layers and staying slow.

Upper body coverage is also requisite since as soon as you feel the asphalt biting into your butt, you'll be anxious to shift to just about any other position. Probably you won't be that controlled and just roll around anyway. So figure on protecting your back. Old leather jackets work pretty well. But you'll probably opt for an old thick sweatshirt that seems 20 times thicker than the long-sleeve tee shirt you were considering. At least until it pulls out of your jeans and rides up your back. Oh, did I mention bringing lots of hydrogen peroxide?

No matter how tempted you are to try street clothes, don't even sit on a board without long sleeves and some kind of gloves. Here is the all too common scenario:

You sit on a new board and think you'll just check out the balance and your ability to lean. The trucks seem like they might be adjusted too tightly. You lie back to get the feel and roll yourself forward about 2 miles an hour. When you lean, instead of turning, the board tips over and you grind big strawberries into the knuckles of one hand. You roll your hand away from the pain and grind your palm also. Later you'll notice your elbow got involved somehow.

While this won't be your worst street luge injury, it will certainly make you feel the stupidest. And later that day, when you do put the gloves on before riding (which you will now never forget) it will really sting.

Stage 2: Jumpsuits

While still discovering how sensitive skin really is, you'll destroy all of your spare clothes. And you'll also be addicted to the rush of gravity's rainbow. Since you need to buy something anyway, it's time to think about getting a little more specialized. If you are ready for some real protection, skip straight to Stage 3. Otherwise, let's make a trip to Army Surplus. Here you find clothes the government designed to beat up. Plus, they have jumpsuits! Which, besides being more aerodynamic, will help prevent your shirt from riding up when you need it most. Duct tape the ankles and pockets closed so they don't balloon at speed. Voila, Cheap Luge Suit!

Other variants in this category include mechanic's coveralls; go-cart suits; and skydiving, cycling, or Lycra outfits over denim (which can be very aero, but offer almost no protection in a high speed crash).

Stage 3: Leathers

After grinding through the butt of your second or third jumpsuit, the extra cost of leathers will begin to make sense. You'll also be looking forward to something that doesn't flop around as much or come in olive drab.

Like most off-the-rack type clothes, ready made leathers will cost much less than custom fitted ones. However, having leathers tailored can also be expensive, so if you are a strange size, skip right to Stage 4. Used leathers could really save you money if they fit. Most motorcycle riders won't have torn their old leathers up too badly before they need to get a new set to match their bigger bike and/or waist line.

There are a few things to look out for when considering motorcycle leathers for street luge. In general, any special road race feature will work against you. Bent knees and elbows are common with good road racing leathers, but you'll be riding with arms and legs straight most of the time. Also, Velcro patches for attaching plastic skid pads will be in the wrong places for luging. They won't hurt, but they cost extra to put there.

The good news is that the more basic the leathers, the less costly they should be and the better suited to your purpose. Do look for reinforced elbows, upper back and butt. Avoid any fancy stitches, joints, colors, letters, etc., across the back that will be more expensive to fix when you scrape them off.

The last decision involves one piece style leathers versus the two piece or jacket/pants types. Most racers have one piece styles with the idea that they are more aero and the top can't ride up in a crash. I would also think that they are less expensive to manufacture as they have fewer panels and zippers. However, I found an inexpensive pair of matching pants and jacket for under $400. They zipper together to prevent separating in a slide, and withstood several years of thrashing. Plus, while everyone else is roasting before a race, I can take the jacket off.

Nevertheless, some racers swear by a one piece design, fearing that the zipper between the pants and jacket could break in a crash. It sounded pretty theoretical to me until I saw a racer with an impressively scarred lower back. He hit a curb with the zippered seam and the jacket pulled up. It's a low probability event, so I'm sticking with my two piece leathers but its something to consider when selecting the quality of your leathers.

Stage 4: Custom Leathers

Welcome to the big time. Where would you like your sponsor's logo? Actually, if you compare the cost of hospital care, lost work time etc., custom leathers make good economic sense, even if you plan to ride conservatively. Plus you have an opportunity to create something really cool.

As mentioned in the Stage 3 discussion, you want a nice trim fit, with straight knees and elbows, a thick back, butt and elbows. You may avoid some of the zippered pockets motorcycle racers use to put in plastic impact pads. Those are for saving your joints in a hard strike to the ground. Not that a catastrophic crash can't happen to you, but your primary concern is frequent sliding. You'll also need impact protection, but probably on the outside of your leathers, so that you don't have to keep having them sewn up. One racing team had Velcro sewn along the forearms and upper back, and then had matching leather segments stuck in place. That way they had double protection and the outer pieces were much cheaper to replace. A neat idea!

Right now, Z-Custom Leathers and Bates have the most experience making luge suits. Both actually have a Street

Luge model, based on the suits they've made for several racers. I had Z make a custom 2 piece set for me with unique colors and lettering. I also had them beef up the areas I destroyed the most quickly on my previous set, add a pocket, and foot stirrups. Plan on spending at least a thousand dollars for custom leathers.

Lots of other great ideas are also out there, some in your own head. Be creative, think about how you'll be using them when going fast, when waiting for a ride up hill, and when crashing at 60 mph. The standards haven't been set yet. The suit doesn't even have to be made of leather. What about combinations of plastic, neoprene, Kevlar, Lycra, and Cordura? There are lots of new materials available today that didn't exist twenty years ago. Have fun designing a second skin to ensure that your first one lasts.

Body Armor

While leathers keep your skin from wearing out, pads can keep your leathers from wearing out. They can also provide additional protection against impact, and you can use them to "feel" the road when turning. If you don't have leathers, you'll need pads so your skin can continue to keep blood inside your body.

Fortunately, because of the in-line skating craze, there are lots of inexpensive pad sets available. Other sports like soccer, hockey, and baseball also offer impact pads that might be adaptable. Eventually street luge will have its own style of body armor but in the mean time, you'll have to improvise.

You might be tempted to forego the knee pads. But even after years of riding, I had a surprise crash while stopping that ate through the knees of my leathers and left scars. At least use knee pads until you are experienced enough to think that you won't crash while stopping, or roll while crashing. This is probably where having pads zippered inside your leathers makes sense. Hopefully, you won't spend much time on your knees, but when you do, you'll be glad the plastic is there. Same for shoulders or other areas that wouldn't touch in a controlled slide, but might be impacted in a tumbling crash.

I have also used soccer shin guards (extra small) to cover my forearms. As scraped up as these have become, it would be nice to have a set that attached directly to the outside of my leathers. I keep wearing through the straps that hold them.

No one has been paralyzed from being "speared" in the back yet, but more and more racers are getting speared and becoming concerned about it. Motorcycle road racers have **spine pads** that protect their vertebrae and it may be time we get on the bandwagon. Another area vulnerable to a strike from a following rider is the back of your neck.

I'm always looking for some type of plastic pads for my butt and upper back. I tend to slide these even while riding well and it would be nice to feel the road in the radical turns without tearing up my leathers.

Shoes

One of the most interesting aspects of street luge involves stopping. Since your feet are your brakes, it pays to spend some time thinking about shoes.

Thin low top canvas shoes are the least expensive and might seem like a good shoe to abuse. Unfortunately, when you go off the road (and you will), you somehow always find a way to grind your ankles and right through the tops of thin shoes. It hurts then and continues to hurt for weeks until the little sores form little scars. The little scars are there to remind you of the value of good shoes.

No one makes specialized street luge shoes yet, but Biker Sherlock is working with Converse™ on a signature shoe that has been beefed up for more protection. Vans™ makes excellent high top shoes for regular skateboarding with flat soles and better ankle protection. When considering shoes, look for a flat sole (no heels), good abrasion protection, and something that will be comfortable pointing your toes (to reduce wind resistance).

Some racers are sponsored by shoe companies. If you aren't, you might think about how to make your shoes last. I watched a 15 year old grind the heels off a $100 pair of tennis shoes in less than 3 runs.

A tried and true method of extending shoe life involves putting old tire tread on the bottom. My first pair of luge shoes were old Nike™ running shoes with tire treads bolted on. Bolting holds the tread tightly to the shoe in a few places and the bolts make really cool sparks when you put your feet down. From a fast stop, the treads smoke like a dragster burnout. And you leave skid marks!

The disadvantage to bolting the treads on is that it's difficult to actually attach them, and some part of a bolt ends up poking into your foot as you walk around. Flush mounting inside the shoe helps with comfort, but you also need a flush mount on the outside so you don't just grind off the end of the bolt and lose the tread. As you stop the bolt gets red hot from grinding and will eventually burn the bottom of your foot. I knew one guy who thought he'd use drywall screws to hold the treads. When he crashed into a hay bale the screws drove into his feet.

A better way to attach the tread is with one of the modern adhesives like Shoe Goo™. Find it at the hardware store, and buy more than you think you'll need. Apply liberally, like a tube per shoe. You won't have a bolt to grind and spark, but the shoes are much easier to build. And the treads will continue to stay on as you wear them out. Be sure to allow ample drying time. The friction from your first stop may be all it takes to break loose any uncured adhesive. I've had treads come off and the remaining glue left foot prints on the street for months.

Experimenting with tread materials can be tricky. Because I had trouble cutting tire, I tried to replace my soles once with sections of a rubber mat. Big mistake. They grabbed, peeled, chattered, and didn't stop as well as plain shoes. I also tried racing tires thinking that since they are so grippy they would help stop me faster. After a few feet of braking they became too grippy and started chattering and sucking my feet under the board. The folks making street car and motorcycle tires have already experimented with the best compounds to grab the road, so I've learned to trust them.

Most service stations will give you an old tire for free. You can make several sets of treads from a single tire so making street luge shoes can be a good group activity. Try to avoid the temptation to keep half a tire laying around for your next set of shoes. It's unsightly, and there is never any good place to store it. I usually have a hunk of tire laying around, thinking that I'm planning ahead. But the shoes invariably last longer than I can put up with the clutter, so I throw away the rest of the tire before I need it. The replacement tire I eventually need is so easy to come by that I wonder why I stored the previous remnants in the first place. And so on. If you want to plan ahead, completely cut out extra pairs of soles, and store them flat somewhere.

Cutting the tire to shape can be an ordeal in itself. A hack saw could work if you had enough patience and strength. A friend of mine cut out a set from a steel belted radial using nothing but tin snips. You need very sharp snips, strong hands, and all day for that one. I once used a chain saw to cut through a cloth belted tire. Not too labor intensive, but very messy and dangerous. After an unsuccessful attempt with a band saw, my latest set came out the cleanest and easiest using a saber saw. Until someone commercially markets special street luge shoes, that's probably my cutting tool of choice. Most guys prefer a cloth belted tire as it is easier to cut and easier on the tools. Soles from steel belted tires leave jagged wires out the sides which tear your clothes and cut your hands mercilessly. However, the little metal wires make cool sparks against the road at night.

I've heard about the possibility of getting retread material from the manufacturer before it is attached to the tire. I haven't tried it yet, but it could be an incredible time saver. Initially cutting away the tire's sidewalls is what takes the most effort. Plus the shoes will last longer as you're not beginning with a worn out tread.

The shape into which you cut the soles is pretty important. My first sets were rectangular, squared off 1" in front and 1" in back of my shoes. The sides were straight and slightly wider than the shoe. Like little water skis. This was partially on the theory that more surface area would help me stop better, and partially because I hadn't yet discovered the saber saw. The treads worked great on the road, but I felt like a clown when walking around.

My friend with the tin snips cut the treads perfectly around his shoes (I still can't believe it). But because he was a beginner, and still dragging his heels, he wore through the back and ruined his shoes anyway. My latest set follow the profile of the shoe and then come straight back 1/2" behind the heel. This allows me some leeway in heel dragging (sometimes it just happens). And the shoes are still comfortable when walking around.

Spare Parts Kit

No discussion of gear would be complete without mentioning spare parts and the tools needed to install them.

The first thing you'll need is a place to put all of the stuff I'm about to mention. Large modular fishing tackle boxes have worked the best for me and my friends. You can get them with lots of separate removable containers, so it's easy to swap smaller parts of your kit in and out, depending upon what you're planning to do. For example, I have one detachable drawer that has only batteries and light bulbs; the specialty stuff for riding at night.

I also have a much larger stackable plastic storage box for things like an extra pair of shoes, extra pads, extra gloves, large lights, big rolls of duct tape—the kinds of things I want to have in the chase car, but won't fit neatly into the tackle box.

In the tackle box I have another removable drawer with just tools. I spent the extra money and bought a separate tool set just for my luge stuff, rather than trying to remember which of my regular tools to bring each time. This way, when I'm ready to go riding, I just grab my Luge box and I know everything is already there. Go over every single nut and screw on your board, wheels, and trucks, and make sure you have a tool to tighten or loosen them. Pieces come loose from vibration and broken pieces will have to be removed and replaced.

After you find all of the wrench sizes and screw driver types to fit your equipment, consider what else might be helpful. I carry a small hammer to help force out bent screws, and a utility knife to cut new padding or tape.

As long as you know what nuts and bolts you use, carry a few extra of these as well. Grade 8 bolts and nylock nuts cut way down on mounting hardware failures, but nothing lasts forever. If a nut comes off that holds your trucks on, you'll need to replace it pronto. Sure you'll have three more, but nuts tend to be like rats leaving a sinking ship. Don't be the last one overboard.

Most avid riders will carry an assortment of bearing sets; ABEC 1s or "thrasher bearings" if they know they will be riding through dirt, mud, and water; ABEC 3s for general riding, and perhaps a set or two of 5s they've saved for racing or the really fast hills. A lot of bearings cycle down from pristine race bearings to thrashers for your next gutter run.

Wheels follow the same life cycle as bearings. New wheels wait for that special speed run when you hope to show up the other riders. After a few runs, you are ready to use them for general riding, and eventually they become scrubbed down enough that you take them off and save them for some time when you know you're going to abuse them. Even then, you'll be tempted to keep them until they're actually destroyed. You still tend to keep a few around for the "You should have seen when this baby came off the hub!" stories. At big races, local kids beg for souvenirs, especially worn down wheels. So plan on stocking at least three sets of wheels besides the ones currently on your board: New racers, extra riders, and thrashers.

I keep a couple of spray cans of lubricant along. WD-40™ or carb cleaner to clean out bearings, and a lubricant to apply afterward. A roll of paper shop towels also helps because things get pretty grimy. Handi-Wipes™ or other "pre-moistened towelettes" are great for keeping the grease on your hands from ending up on your face. A smattering of adhesives can also save a trip. I'll carry Loc-Tite™, Shoe Goo™, and Super-Glue™ with the hope that noncritical equipment may be temporarily kept together.

Some things, like extra gloves, or even extra shoe laces may seem overkill until you are hours from home and need them to keep riding. An extra face shield can also come in handy when yours becomes too scratched up to use. And if you ride with a tinted shield, have a clear one available in case you are still riding as the sun goes down.

First Aid Kit

In scuba diving, almost everyone carries a first aid kit, and aside from decongestants, rarely is it needed. Skydivers don't prepare for first aid, they figure 911 or nothing. Street lugers rarely carry first aid, but need it frequently.

Unfortunately, three recent luge safaris ended in the Emergency waiting room waiting for a fallen buddy, and all trips required that I administer first aid prior to transport.

This seems to take the wind out of my "Not Insanely Dangerous" intro, but I still have to hold to it. The sport is not "Insanely" dangerous—meaning you don't have to be insane to participate. However, you are in denial if you don't accept the inherent dangers of any sport and prepare for them. The first recent trip to E.R. was because of a hidden storm drain that would have killed a bicyclist or in-line skater. The second event involved the rider playing around with the vehicle filming him. The third accident occurred when a buddy went into a cattle grate we were anticipating and snapped his leg anyway. And I really want to hurry and finish this book before I have any more horrendous anecdotes to share.

I didn't have to save anyone's life, and they were all back riding shortly, but I was awfully glad I had something constructive to do during those first tense minutes.

Since this is an abrasion based sport, that is really where you need to concentrate. Sure, you could get snake bit on the side of the road, but an asphalt bite is much more likely. Sure, I've seen several broken fingers, but I haven't taken to carrying splints either. What you need is sterile gauze, tape, and Telfa pads. Even sprains can wait until you get back to town for ice.

I carry little packets of antibiotic ointment and a bottle of hydrogen peroxide in the car. One of the attending doctors said he preferred washing scrapes with plain water. Depending on how you plan to treat scrapes, have that method immediately available.

I'm not going to dispense expert advise on first aid. If you haven't yet taken a course on first aid, I can't recommend it highly enough. Even ask your doctor. Become an expert on treating abrasions. And carry what's necessary. The first bad accident this season was miles from any car (we were dropped off at the top of a closed road and planned to meet the car 9 miles below). In a fit of boy scout preparation, I duct taped first aid stuff directly to my board. Most of the time I feel like a worrisome mother for carrying first aid. But this time, I was ready for a merit badge after stopping the stream of blood that gushed from my buddy's slit throat onto his leathers.

The lesson:

Don't be caught by the side of the road with nothing but sympathy in your heart and tears in your eyes.

Choosing Appropriate Runs

In the beginning, I talked about how street luge was not totally illegal or insanely dangerous, but you could make it that way by riding like a reckless moron. You can also ride very carefully down an inappropriate road and also be a moron. I know, because I have been a moron many times in the past, helping keep the sport in the dark ages for almost 20 years. Most veterans have been. Sorry.

The easiest rule of thumb for choosing a run is not violating its initial purpose. Roads closed for a luge race are very good. Steep freeways are very bad. Crowded running paths are bad. If the road was meant for vehicle traffic and you interfere with that traffic then you are a jerk. Just like the bicycle morons who bomb our courses when they have been blocked off for a luge race.

Right now, aside from sporadic races, there are no dedicated street luge venues so we must find other places to ride where we will be tolerated. That usually means streets (hence the "street" luge title). Pick one carefully. Above all other considerations, your life may depend on it.

Chase Car

If you choose to ride on a road that is open to traffic, you are taking the additional risk of being run over by a car. You are small and below the line of sight for most vehicles, and we know from driving that most people don't pay attention.

You can attach a flag pole to your luge (like they do with children's bicycles) to increase your visibility. It will slow you down a little, but open roads aren't for racing anyway. However, my concern is not for the cars that don't see me, but for the one's that do and act inappropriately.

The **chase car** is usually the vehicle that transported you to the top of the hill in the first place. Its job isn't so much to chase you down the hill as it is to block cars from running you over from behind.

The normal public always worries about the cars coming at you in the uphill lane. You have a fast closing speed, and the oncoming drivers are usually surprised when they see you. As long as you stay on your side, they aren't a problem. Even if they came in your lane and tried to force a head-on collision, you'd see them and could squirt by in the gutter.

No, your big worry is the cars already on your side of the road. The ones in front usually aren't a problem if you slow down and maintain a large gap. If the driver finally notices you in the rear view mirror, they will either slow down to watch or panic and slam on the brakes. Either way they become a hazard. The way to avoid these confrontations is to let all traffic clear before going down the hill.

This leaves the very real hazard of being overtaken by cars from behind. Your ability to turn fast doesn't help, because you won't see them coming. Your ability to stop quickly is a detriment, because it will just put you under their tires all the faster. What you need is to keep these cars off your tail, and a good chase car driver should do just that. The chase driver should know how quickly you can stop and where you are likely to do so. They'll block traffic from behind and keep a good safe distance so they don't run you over first.

A chase car means you need to be able to coast the speed limit. If you go too slowly, cars will stack up behind the chase vehicle, get pissed off, and try to pass. When they come zooming around and back into their lane, imagine how surprised they'll be as you go under their wheels.

If you go too fast, the chase car won't be able to keep up, and will be risking a speeding ticket if they try. If you get a testosterone overflow and start overtaking cars in your lane, the chase car will be left behind. And now you're unprotected again. Great.

I heard a horrendous story about a guy who was going too fast and dropped the chase car. An amazed spectator in a mini-truck decided to keep up and watch. When the rider overtook and passed another car in his lane, the mini-truck lost sight of him and also went for the pass. Pulling back into the lane, he hit the rider who spun around and went underneath. Lodged backward, injured, but still on his board, the rider looked for a way to slide out under the differential of the speeding truck. Unfortunately, the driver realized he had the luger underneath and swerved, running him over seriously a second time. (The rider lived but was severely injured.)

Don't leave the chase car!

Scouting Hills

Every great road is an intersection of the things you require and an absence of the things you cannot tolerate. And it is never at the intersection of another road.

Many roads look promising at a distance, but turn out to have some disqualifying factor when you get there. Scouting for hills while driving around will become an obsession as you get more into the sport. Every time you drive by a hilly region, your mental gauge will be saying, "Hey, that looks like it has potential!"

Asking other people if they know of good hills can really reduce your scouting time. Maps help somewhat but local people's experience will point you to the best possibilities sooner.

Things you require from a road are:
- Adequate Steepness
- Sufficient Distance
- Sufficient Run Out
- Rideable Surface
- Good Visibility
- Minimal Traffic

Watch Downhill Speed

Geographically flat areas will not have any good hills. But flat is relative, and even small rolling hills can provide fun rides. Major mountain passes will have the best vertical drops, but the road selections are usually limited. If the one road down the hill is too rough, or too travelled, the whole area is out.

If you can coast the speed limit in a car, then the road is probably steep enough for luge. If it's much slower, you will hold up traffic and have to worry about getting run over by the cars behind you.

Searching for road signs is like big game hunting. "Watch Downhill Speed" is a good indicator that the road will be steep enough to ride. "6% grade" or "Use Low Gear" will also accompany roads that meet the steepness test. Again, coasting the hill in another vehicle first is the best way to find out.

Some roads are too steep. The EDI Lake Elsinore Grand Prix has been held on Tuscany Hill* that makes Signal Hill* look like a bunny slope. The pro course is only 35 seconds long. You are going over 70 mph as you find out how well your board will hold the right sweeper after the bump. Drifting out and hitting the hay bales at those speeds can be devastating.

---

*These are racer's names for the hills and not the actual street names.

Years before the first race at Elsinore, local resident Bob Price brought me to the hill and dared me to ride[†]. After I rocketed down, Bob said he knew of a really extreme hill that was too steep to ride.

At the time I didn't believe in "too steep," but Bob's find was the 27% Grade. If you're a newbie you probably don't realize that a 6% grade is very fast and a 10% grade is crazy fast. A signed 27% grade is like hooking a fish that's way bigger than the boat.

I've only taken a few experienced riders to the 27% Grade; riders I trusted to use good judgement. Half opted not to attempt it. Of the half that did try, half of those crashed and couldn't ride anymore that day.

On this road there are off-camber, bumpy turns that are so steep you are accelerating under full brakes. For nearly a mile, you have to choose between fighting the acceleration and trying to make the turns. If you go into these turns with any speed it all, you will crash. It's a **double black diamond run** and really isn't much fun. You start at the top and try to survive getting to the bottom. Even losing a tread from your shoe would mean almost certain injury.

In our travels, we've found other unsigned hills that none of us would attempt. I don't know how steep they were, but once you discover acceleration under full brakes you too will believe in "too steep."

Minimal Length

Short hills are good if you plan on walking back up. Sometimes walking is a necessity (or recommended if you're brand new) but a lift sure is nice. If you have a ride back up the hill, about 1/2 mile will seem the shortest distance that

---

† I would NEVER ride the hill now unless it's a permitted event. Once a city agrees to let us race a hill it's TOTALLY TABOO to pre-ride and risk the permit. If a city wants to keep us off a hill, they can make it an annual event and everyone will avoid it the other 364 days.

is worth while. Many luge race courses are that short and the whole thing is over in under a minute. At some point, short hills are like an amusement park: You wait and wait and then boom, it's over.

Long hills are anything over 3 to 4 miles. I'm pulling specific numbers out of my hat, but many riders probably feel the same way. Personally, I like long hills. They physically wear some guys out, and the longer you go, the more likely your wheels will melt and fail. Nevertheless, getting on your luge and coasting for miles and miles is an unparalleled joy. Racing your friends on a long road means you can blow a few turns, still catch up, and pass them. My longest continuous run is about 14 miles with two stops for cattle grates.

Medium hills are about 2 miles long, which seems to be the magic distance. It's long enough that you get to ride for a few minutes between loading and unloading the truck. It's not so long that you unexpectedly wear out your equipment or your stomach. If someone finds a new 2 mile road, I'm ready to ride.

Where Will You Stop?

The steepest, longest hill in the world is no good if there isn't adequate room to stop at the end. I've found really tempting hills that were immediately disqualified because you would still be accelerating as you ran smack into a curb, road block, or intersection.

The final braking area is called **run out** and the absolute best run outs are uphill. That takes away the pressure of hard braking. There is little more satisfying than nailing a speedy run and then flying uphill screaming "Whooo!"

Flat sections are also good for run outs, but make sure the surface isn't dirty or bumpy, or you will skid a lot longer than you anticipate. One of the most surprising injuries I received was while braking on a dirty run out. My shoes were slowing me effectively and then started to slip on the sand. I applied more pressure. Suddenly I hit a clean patch of road and both of my feet stuck and sucked under the board. I ended up straddling the board on both knees and ground through the leathers into my knee caps. I couldn't have been going more than 10 mph.

A lot of run outs are really "peter-outs," where the road gradually becomes less steep, and you can't keep up enough speed to make it worth continuing. Those sections can be valuable, because as you get faster you will be able to ride further on the road and measure your progress.

On race courses, the run out is frequently referred to as the **shut down grid**. You hear a lot about how quickly luge racers can stop and people come to depend on it. To save the amount of road that has to be blocked off, promoters will minimize the length of the shut down grid and line the end of the course with hay bales. It can be an exciting place to watch as the racers come flying across the finish line and immediately start smoking their shoes. Guys will start pulling Show Stoppers* and a couple will stumble and eat it. A few racers will blow the grid and continue skidding into the hay bales at the end. In the interest of safety, the grid will be extended until all the racers can make it.

Short run outs on open roads can be a necessity, but that means you will always have to hold back and slow early. Because you are skidding your shoes, your braking distance will not be as consistent as you might expect. The temptation to race with your friends eventually becomes a game of "chicken," each guy braking later and later, until someone loses a tread, and you all go to the hospital. Real roads don't end in hay bales.

*This technique is described under *Braking*

Clearly defined, adequate braking areas really make a road fun. If there isn't adequate run out, move on down the road and find a place that does.

Smooth is Good

If a hill isn't smoothly paved, it will be hard to turn and stop. It will also be much slower, and will chew up your wheels. Rough pavement is also dangerous and isn't even fun.

Roads that are rough but rideable will feel much faster than their smooth counterparts. Speed estimates go up about 10 mph on rough roads, because the riders work harder to hold the turns and vibration goes way up.

Rougher roads are very dangerous to fall onto. Just as coarse sand paper works faster, a rough road will go through your thickest leathers in a hurry. In some parts of the country, roads are purposely repaved with a rough texture which ruins them for luge.

I can't really come up with a definition of "too rough." However, I can tell you that smooth, newly paved roads are heavenly. Veteran riders have favorite sites they no longer ride because the road surface degrades. Years later they call and say, "You'll never believe it, but they repaved our road!"

Driveways & Intersections

Back when I was immortal, I rode on steep residential streets. There are a lot of them out there. And sometimes it was fun. With all the driveways, the road is like those combat shooting ranges where something unexpected keeps popping up to kill you.

I don't ride residential roads any longer. And not so much because I'm worried about someone backing into me. The residents believe they will back into me, or I will kill their children playing in the street; or maybe they just resent having strangers use their neighborhood as a playground. So I find other, better roads on which to ride. Plus, no one will have a future race on residential roads; too many people to make happy.

A run that requires crossing an intersection is also undesirable. If it's a stop sign, you have to stop or you'll be breaking the law. You have to worry about cops seeing you, or cars killing you. Not worth it. At all. Start blowing through stop signs and your days of street luge are seriously numbered.

Lighted intersections are also a gamble. If the light is green, the run goes on. Red—and the run comes to an end. Plus the cars that are stopped behind will out accelerate you, and you'll have exposure to being run over from behind. Run the light, and it's Russian roulette. If you think you can time the light and look for cars, make out a will now. Include a "please unplug me from the heart/lung/kidney/drool machine" clause.

Or avoid intersections and driveways all together. Please.

Traffic Patterns

Roads that are great at one time of day can suck another time. This sounds like it works against you, but if you plan right, it's really advantageous.

Business parks are the best example. There is way too much traffic to ride the roads in business parks during the week. During the weekend, most business parks are pretty deserted.

Mountain roads can be just the opposite. During the week, hardly anyone travels up to resort areas, but the weekend turns them into raceways. If you hope to avoid cars, recreational roads need to be approached during normal business hours when most people are at work.

In all cases, plan to ride when the roads have the lowest traffic patterns. And remember that any road which is not closed has potential motorists lurking around the next corner.

Hidden Dangers

Cars are the obvious danger on any road. Next to cars come guard rails and cliffs. There are quite a few obvious hazards. But sometimes it's the hidden obstacles that present the greatest danger.

My teammate, Dave Auld, and I went to a bike path to teach a new rider how to luge. We figured the bike path would be ideal as it was under 30 mph and there would be no cars. As we cruised under a foot bridge, a couple walking their dogs stopped in the middle of the path. Dave slammed on the brakes but the path was wet and he kept sliding into the tunnel. Finally the couple split and both moved to either wall. Dave started to spin and came off his board. As I passed him, helpless under the tangle of leashes, the dogs attacked.

Other animal hazards exist on forested roads. I have heard of riders hitting wild dogs, rabbits, squirrels, raccoons, and poisonous snakes. It's not the same thump as when your car rolls over some helpless creature. These animals are frightened and injured as they come bouncing into your face at 40 mph.

City streets have parked cars, which come un-parked at inopportune times. People get out of them right in front of you. There are also man hole covers which won't affect a car, but will bust a skateboard wheel right off. Storm drains run along the gutter and don't seem like a hazard unless you think about sliding half way into one at speed.

Country roads don't have concrete curbs to hit. When you go off pavement, you usually skid along the dirt and weeds until you stop. It seems pretty innocuous and usually is. But keep in mind that the dirt and weeds hide all sort of nasty discarded hazards like holes, boulders, or rusty metal frames. Trees sway in the breeze and don't look so solid or dangerous. But they might as well be concrete if you hit one. Country roads also have cattle grates which will snap your legs or arms if you try to ride across one. A barbed wire fence will slice you like cheese if you slide off the road and go through one.

Inspect all runs thoroughly before riding them. Even if we have ridden a road a hundred times before, we always take a car from the top to the bottom before every new day of riding. Walk the road if it's closed to traffic. Consider bringing a broom so you can clean off dirty sections that interfere with braking. Check for rocks that litter mountain roads or any new debris deposited by rain runoff. Make sure there are no new unexpected surprises.

Learning to Ride

You will always be learning about new equipment and new techniques. On your first day out *be cautious.* You don't have to go 50 mph but you can. You don't have to crash, but many do.

Your best bet is to start with a board that an experienced rider has ridden and can verify was set up correctly. There are a lot of subtleties that add up to a board appearing fine but becoming uncontrollable at speed. If a board doesn't work, beginning riders will keep crashing and blaming themselves for the accident.

After putting on some protective gear, get used to the board by having someone push you across flat ground. Make sure it turns properly. Even experts can mistakenly put a set of trucks on backward; which means — lean left and the board turns right out from under you! The last thing you want to do is drive out to some cool hill with an untested board, only to find 10 yards into the run that it needs to go back to the garage for quick but fundamental changes.

Any time I make big changes to my boards I'll roll across the driveway and ask myself, "How well can I still brake? Do these changes interfere with my ability to turn?" Make sure you have the braking motions down. Don't wait to try stopping until you are already afraid of the speed. Most accidents come from panic reactions and not from equipment failure. Master your skills thoroughly at slow speed and your high speed reactions will be there when you need them.

What's Fast?

When you are learning to ride, make sure you don't try to go too fast. Fast is a relative term so let me give you my take on the various speeds:

Under 10 mph is slow. The board probably won't handle very well but you will still get hurt if you tip over without proper protection.

20 mph starts to be really fun. It's faster than you can run and you'll get a good feel for what the sport is about.

30-50 mph is legitimate Street Luge. Depending on the type of hill, this may be all the speed you'll ever want or need. Really twisty courses max out at these speeds because the board is sliding through the turns. Narrow paths will seem unbelievably fast at these speeds.

50-60 mph is the golden range for experts. We're talking freeway speeds on skateboard! Even on straight roads, over 50 is fun for an expert. Things start to click and aerodynamics become very important. Most beginners can get up to these speeds but will be on the outside of their ability to control the board and will unexpectedly wipe out.

60-70 mph always feels fast. Experts need a really steep, smooth road to get much over 60. Rough roads feel much faster but even the steepest inevitably top out here. Wheels start melting at these speeds and even full leathers offer marginal protection.

70-80 mph is adrenaline city! If the hill isn't really scary coasting in a car then you won't hit 70 on a luge. Very few roads in the world offer these speeds and going this fast is always illegal.* Most experts have gone over 70 mph, although not as often as they think. Even a slight change in foot position will pull you around a turn. Riding at over 70 mph requires 100% concentration: Hold on to the tightest tuck and pray your wheels don't explode.

---

*unless it's a permitted event

Over 80 mph, the mythical barrier. Roger Hickey set a Guinness World Record at 78 mph on a specialized luge designed specifically for speed runs. Several riders (including Roger) have unofficially broken 80 mph on more conventional boards. Once, my reliable, on-board speedometer showed 81.5 mph after a perfect run down a very long steep smooth hill. The next day, with different weather conditions, I couldn't get out of the high 70s.

Top speeds are fickle and change hour to hour on the same hill. That's why I prefer races to records when deciding who's fast. Ultra high speed may sound like something to shoot for but it's really more dangerous than fun. I can't imagine escaping catastrophic injury when your equipment fails. And at ultra high speeds—it will fail.

There is a certain velocity at which the human body will *pick up and fly* before stalling and crashing back to the ground. Over 80 felt like I was approaching that speed.

Your First Hill

Your first hill doesn't need to be fast—in fact it shouldn't be! Riding fast hills before you are ready is dangerous and will teach you bad habits. Practicing on slow hills will encourage you to try to get every mph out of them.

First, get someone to push you around someplace flat so you can convince yourself that you will be able to turn and stop this thing. And don't pick someplace stupid like a busy parking lot where you'll get run over. After you've mastered the flat land, pick a short, gradual hill with **NO TRAFFIC**. Find a baby hill.

A big problem for beginners is "Target Fixation." You see something bad and instead of turning away, you stare at it until you collide. Remember the parachutist's motto: **Look Away—Turn Away**. For us this means concentrating on where we need to go; not watching a hazard until we run into it. No matter how large a car is, it can't take up the entire road. You can almost always slow down or go around. But it will take a while to build the appropriate reactions, so beginners need to completely avoid traffic. A closed road, park, or private property (with permission) would be ideal.

Your first baby hill should be so short that you can walk back up. Ride down to the bottom; drag the board back up to the top. It sounds strange, but if you start off with a truckload of experienced riders they will inadvertently pressure you to "Hurry up" or "Go faster." You need to build your confidence gradually until you honestly feel "This baby hill sucks!"

This is no time to give into peer pressure. It's not like smoking, which takes many years to kill you. You can be severely injured and die by riding a hill for which you are not prepared. Impress your friends later by developing solid riding skills now. Don't be their crash test dummy.

If your experienced friends want to ride the hill instead of watch and lecture you, it's probably too steep. To gauge the speed of little hills you can always coast down on a bicycle beforehand.

You first "Real Hill" involves getting rides back up. It should be in the 20-30 mph range. No traffic. No obstacles. No hard turns. Experienced riders should be willing to take a few runs with you and check on your style. Play around and get confident with your equipment. Don't run into anything stationary. Now is the time to start learning how to brake and how to turn.

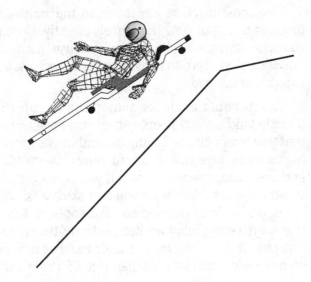

You can be severely injured and die
by riding a hill for which you are not prepared.

Braking

On a steep enough grade, anyone can get a street luge traveling over 60 mph. Slowing safely from that speed is another matter.

Mechanical Brakes

Most people are appalled that luge racers use their feet to stop, rather than a sophisticated set of mechanical brakes. However, experienced riders are equally reluctant to rely on mechanical systems, particularly if it prevents them from using their feet. Here's why:

The most obvious approach to mechanized brakes involves trying to slow the wheels directly. Cars, bicycles, go-carts—almost everything on wheels use this method. But skateboard wheels don't have any good place against which to rub a brake pad.

If you could engineer something to rub the wheel directly (and several people have) you have to remember that you won't just be rolling around in your driveway. At high speeds, luge wheels are turning close to 10,000 rpm and urethane is prone to melt. If you could get the brakes to slow the wheels, they'll want to skid, wash out in the turns, and quickly develop bad flat spots. Not to mention that even if everything worked perfectly, the contact patch (the part of the wheel that actually touches the road) of all your wheels is still smaller than that of a single shoe.

The easiest and most widely attempted method of mechanical braking is to imitate the shoe, and force a large brake pad directly against the ground. This method overcomes the difficulty involved with trying to stop the wheels directly, and can offer a contact patch as large as necessary. I've seen some nice examples ranging from hand levers to "stomp on it" brake peddles. And they can all slow you down fast; but only in a straight line.

There is one major problem with placing a brake pad under the luge. The same force pushing down against the road also pushes the luge and its wheels into the air. When the weight lifts off the wheels they won't turn effectively and the reason you usually need to slow down is because you're already going too fast to make the next corner.

So experienced riders still drag their feet, leaving skid marks and blue smoke while their treads burn around the high speed turns.

Technique

Once you've accepted that your feet can and will be used to stop, braking technique is what will stop you in time.

Street luge braking is more complicated than mechanical braking where you can just push a lever harder to stop faster. There are stages to braking and not everyone does it exactly the same way.

The most gentle and tentative form is to tap a heel. This assures you that the ground is still there. If you need to slow down just a little, this is the preferred method without changing your position on the luge. If you want to save your shoes, you can sit up a little, which uses air resistance to slow you down and gives you better visibility. I'll combine these techniques when going into an unfamiliar turn or any time there shouldn't be cars lurking around, but might be.

If you need to slow more strongly, say for a tight turn, you should start by dragging a foot. This means gradually bringing your foot back from the pegs, dragging a heel, and then rolling your foot forward. Bend your knee so you can slide on the entire bottom of your shoe. If you don't roll your foot forward, you will quickly burn through the heel of the shoes and into the heel of your foot.

Keep in mind, the key to effective braking is a gradual rolling motion. If you just slam your foot down hard, it will tend to chatter and jam back on you. Easy does it. If your shoes do chatter during braking, ease up on the pressure until they start sliding and then gradually reapply pressure.

If I'm trying to slow through a corner, I'll brake with my outside foot and leave my inside leg free to help control the turn. You *can* brake with the inside leg instead, and sometimes there is good reason to do so. But braking with the outside foot is helpful because pushing on the outside of the turn helps you lean inward more easily. Prove this to yourself by practicing ahead of time while the board is sitting still.

Heavy braking requires the full bottoms of both your feet. Bend your knees and arch your hips to put more weight on your feet. Keep in mind, this un-weights your front wheels, hindering your ability to turn. It will also test the stability of your board, so try heavy braking from slow speeds at first. Build up progressively to faster and faster speeds.

Some people like to sit up under full braking, which signals to other riders that they are stopping. Sitting up also supplies additional air resistance. It also allows them to pull up on the board, putting even more downward force to their feet.

Heavy braking will smoke your shoes and leave impressive skid marks. But to really impress your friends, try a standing stop, otherwise known as the **"Show Stopper."**

A show stopper is where you pull the nose of your board high into the air and skid in a squatting position. Because all the weight is on your shoes, smoke will billow off the treads. Plus if you build a spear board it will look like you're holding a giant boner.

Your shoes will heat up rapidly and develop extra traction. When you eventually lose your balance, your feet will suck under and you'll come crashing down hard on your face. Breaking while braking. Cool.

Turning

Just like braking, turning is done differently to different degrees and not everyone's technique is the same. The most important thing is to MAKE IT AROUND THE CORNER. And let me reiterate: On a street luge, if you are braking hard, you cannot turn hard at the same time. I've seen too many riders give up on turning and brake straight into a hay bale, guard rail, or side of a mountain. Learn how to accomplish hard sliding turns before trying to go fast.

Basic turning is amazingly simple. Since these are skateboards, you only have to put more weight on the side to which you wish to turn. On a well tuned board it will seem like mental telepathy. Tip your head to one side and your board should follow along. At speed, for gradual turns, that's all it should take. On certain boards you can do the same thing by slightly shifting your hips.

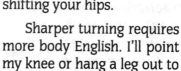

Sit up slightly

Sharper turning requires more body English. I'll point my knee or hang a leg out to turn in that direction. Or I'll drop a shoulder off. Or both a leg and a shoulder. Both the weight shift and aerodynamic drag help you around the turn. Some guys like to sit up higher for better leverage, others like to keep their backs flat and almost drag them along the road. There are a lot more techniques available on a street luge than any other vehicle.

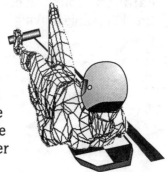

Drag the outside foot

There is one major functional difference between laying down on a long skateboard and riding a street luge. The foot pegs on a luge can do much more than just hold up your feet. The lean that helps you around a corner will also try to tip your outside wheels in to the air. That means less traction.

Shift head & shoulders

However, by applying downward force to the foot peg, you can keep the wheels more firmly planted and get better traction. Depending on the twist (torsional flex) of your finished board, you may find that pressure to the inside or outside peg will help you around.

As I mentioned, the normal technique used for heavy braking is contrary to heavy turning. Heavy braking shifts the weight away from your wheels and on to your shoes; and your shoes don't turn. But there is a way to slow when you find yourself already in a corner going way too

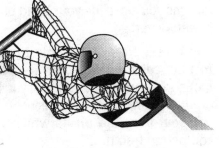

Use inside leg for leverage

fast. It's at the wilder side of turning technique and is a difficult yet important skill to master. It's sliding.

Sliding

While learning how sharply you can reliably turn, you will eventually induce a slide. It's not the desired way around a corner, but it's a technique you can use to your advantage.

Suppose you're flying down a road which has turns you've insufficiently memorized. You set up for a 50 mph sweeping right hander and YIPES . . . the guard rail hooks sharply to the left instead–a hairpin turn. And if you slam on the brakes now, there's not enough room to brake in a straight line! You're going way too fast to hold the turn. You'll have to try **sliding**.

Sliding is turning and slowing simultaneously. Before you accept going into a guard rail, at least try to crank your luge as far as it will go. **Slide the wheels around and away.**

Going into a really sharp corner, start by braking with your outside foot and keep it flat around the turn. Sit up a little and shift your shoulders to the inside of the turn. Point your inside leg to where you need to go. Make your body into a big crescent flowing toward the inside of the turn. Pull up on the board with your outside hand. On some designs you can slide your hand back on the board for even greater leverage.

To really crank a panic turn, I've done everything mentioned plus dragged my back and shoulders, my inside foot and my inside hand too. If you have to, drag everything around the inside of a surprisingly sharp turn and help pivot the board around on its wheels. Refuse to learn about compound fractures.

After you get really good at sliding you can use it as a technique to discover how fast a turn can be taken. The top experts can fly into some sharp turns without pre-applying brakes, using the slide itself to slow down. They also know how to maintain the fine balance between the slide and the traction needed to make the corner. Eventually they figure out how fast they can take the corner without sliding and how much braking should be used to set up for the turn.

It takes a tremendous amount of sliding experience to weigh all the variables. Every board slides differently. Each make and model of wheel behave in a different manner. Individual sets of wheels transform as they wear down. Road surfaces change everything. Even temperature makes a difference.

Controlling the balance between slide and traction is an art. When you get good at sliding, you can let your board drift into a turn, keeping your weight evenly distributed; then apply downward pressure on the pegs to re-gain front traction and stop the slide. If you do it correctly, you'll carry a lot more speed out of the turn than you would by sliding through. Just be careful how soon you try to override a natural slide. Apply pressure too soon and you can high-side a luge just like a motorcycle.

Practice cutting slides short little by little. After you have mastered allowing the board to come out of the slide on it's own, gradually learn how much peg pressure you can apply and how soon to apply it. Sliding 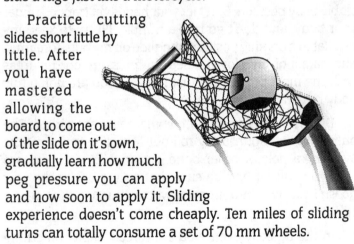 experience doesn't come cheaply. Ten miles of sliding turns can totally consume a set of 70 mm wheels.

Crashing

Eventually it happens with everything. Take enough showers, you'll slip in the tub. Take up this sport; you will scrape up your leathers.

There are essentially two types of crash to prepare for. One where you come off the board and your body slides to a stop. The other where you and your board collide with a stationary object. You can dress for the first type of accident, but until we have airbag fairings, I would avoid hitting anything solid.

If you come off the board at speed, the good news is you will eventually stop. While waiting for that to happen there are things you can do to minimize or even totally escape injury. The first of those things happened before you ever get on the board; **Buy good gear**. There is nothing like grinding into your underwear during the first 2 seconds of a 5 second slide!

The next important thing is to maintain a wide, flat, stable body position. Don't let your hands get trapped under your body, and don't go into a tumble. I'll try to keep my feet flat in a braking position and slide on my butt, forearms, and palms of my gloves. Keep the pressure on the areas with the most protection. Just imagine you are doing full-body braking.

Do what you can to watch where you are sliding. The only time I will purposely roll out of a slide is if it means avoiding a pole or other bone buster. Wait until you are sure you will hit and be sure that rolling out of the way doesn't put you into an even worse situation (like over a cliff).

In the unlikely event you are forced to hit something solid, remember that force is measured in pounds per square inch. There is not much you can do to shed pounds just before impact (although your body will try). You may have some ability to spread the impact over the largest possible area. Hit something big and flat versus small and sharp. Take the impact with the whole right side of your body versus just your right wrist. If you can distribute the impact over time with a hit-and-roll type technique, you lessen the severity of the impact even more. Like they say, "It's not the fall that kills the jumper, it's the sudden stop at the end." Keep your stops *gradual.*

In the martial arts, they teach a sitting fall where you hit first on your butt; then roll more to your back; hit on your forearms, then hands. The motion is fluid and coordinated timing is important. You can't learn technique like that from a book, but the idea of impact distribution applies.

Parachuting teaches the PLF (Parachute Landing Fall). The idea is to lessen the impact of hitting the ground feet first, when falling too fast. It has dynamics similar to what we go through when hitting something in front of us.

The PLF technique is where you strike the ground first with your legs (absorbing most of the impact) then roll off to one side, distributing the impact to the side of the calf, thigh, butt, and shoulder. The recommendation is to keep the hands and elbows forward and in tight to the chest so they don't get broken.

You can practice the PLF by jumping off a small platform onto soft ground. Being comfortable with the technique could come in handy in a future accident. You can also get carried away with simulation and not be able to luge because you broke your legs jumping off the garage.

Since sliding along the ground without your luge means potential injury, and hitting something solid means almost certain injury, always choose the former. If you lose control of your board and it's about to rocket you into something solid, bail off immediately. You will probably hit anyway but at a much slower speed.

If you are sliding and braking with your outside foot, don't let that foot get trapped between the board and whatever you're sliding into. Pick up your leg before impact. Your board can quickly become your worst enemy in a crash.

One last quick note. **Hay bales** that line race courses **are not soft.** Racers that hit them at speed can and do break bones. Frequently. At high speed you can die hitting hay bales. The techniques of impact distribution are just as important with hay bales as they are with other stationary objects. My best advice is—until you are absolutely sure of any course, slow down. **Use your brakes; don't hit anything.**

Drafting

Behind every rider is an invisible pocket of air. Within this pocket is the secret to increased speed.

Anytime you follow another pilot, there is less air resistance than when riding alone. The air displaced by the lead rider means you can achieve a burst of acceleration by closing in behind them, and passing at the last moment. As the diagram at the left suggests, the draft becomes more effective as you get closer to the rider's head. Too far back or to the side, and you miss the benefit of the draft. And the size of the drafting envelope increases with the speed of the lead rider.

Street luge involves even more timing and technique than other sports which utilize the draft. With powered vehicles, racers can "rest" in the draft and time a pass for the critical moment. With gravity sports, the draft must be taken advantage of as the rider enters the envelope. If the pass is too early on the course, the overtaken rider will draft the new leader and re-pass later on. Or by waiting, the trailing rider will be forced to brake instead of passing, losing the brief acceleration the initial draft provided.

When racing, the timing of a draft move is critical to the final results. On fun rides, cycling through drafting leaders can improve the pace of the entire run, and provide experience in close quarters maneuvering.

Following and Leading

An interesting fact about luge accidents is that they rarely involve a following rider. It's almost always the lead or solo rider that goes in. I have a few theories about why this happens.

First, the lead rider is probably leading because he is going faster than anyone else. Hopefully this additional speed is warranted by superior skill and knowledge *of that hill.* When it isn't — look out.

Second, the lead rider doesn't have as many clues as to what lies in the road ahead. Following riders can watch the reactions of the lead and brake sooner or have more time to change their line. Plus, if the lead rider spins out in a turn, he can look forward to being speared by everyone behind him.

Following another rider is not only safer than leading, it's more interesting. You can watch and learn from their moves, try to improve on their lines. Sneak a little draft and then back off. Plus you get to watch luge and do it at the same time.

If I'm racing someone who knows a twisty course better than I do, I'll follow them down. Even if I think I'm faster, I'm reluctant to try an early pass. I'll follow and wait for them to make a mistake. If the pressure of racing causes them to blow a turn, I can cruise the rest of the course at a comfortable pace. If they have a clean run and it turns out I am faster, I can always try a pass at the end of the course. Otherwise, I'll come in second, but in one piece. I might not always win, but at least I won't jump ahead early and go piling into the hay bales on a surprise corner.

If you're an overly aggressive new rider, you will naturally develop a "newbie etiquette" that will drive the experienced riders crazy. When you're just riding for fun with someone, follow them all the way down a technical run. Always make the "finish line" a few feet further than where they start slowing. In the last few yards, when they sit up to brake, whip past them and then throw your arms into the air like you've just won some important championship. (It's really awesome if this causes you to lose your balance and crash.) Later, keep referring to how you "beat them" on that run. When they remind you that it's not a race, remark, "That's OK. I still won." The next time down, the angry leader will try to shake you off their tail. One easy way is by riding really closely to rocks or potholes that the following rider (you) won't see in time to avoid. If you piss off the person you're following, you'll probably bend an axle or crash. So bring extra equipment and first aid. Or curb your desire to treat fun rides like races.

There is also a distinction between following and trying to keep up. Don't try holding on to a rider that seems to be going too fast. They may have much better braking or sliding skills and can go into a turn hotter than you can. They may have a better handling board. Or they might be nuts and lead the both of you, sliding, over the side of a cliff.

If you follow someone of your same ability, it will seem slower than if you were riding alone. If you are following and begin to feel like you are going too fast — you are. Back off and let them go.

Don't get in over your head.

Sometimes you follow not out of good judgement, but because you are just too slow to keep up. Even if the lead rider is not immediately visible, they will leave you telltale clues about the corners. **Look for skid marks. Smell for smoke.** If I'm way behind on a twisty road, I'm sniffing for burning rubber like a hound. When I smell it, I know to slow down and look for the braking point.

Riding Styles

The '95 Extreme Games brought riders together from various parts of the world. Of particular note were the German riders, who attacked the sharp city corners in a manner different from the Americans present. Quickly the announcers picked up on the different techniques and labeled one the "German" style.

Watching at home, many of us who raced mountain switchbacks also recognized the technique. We didn't learn it from the Germans, nor had they ever seen us ride. Rather than being regional, the technique is used by riders who are used to negotiating very sharp turns. The technique used by the group of Americans at the games had been developed for the faster sweeping turns *they* had learned on.

Having come from a background which emphasized mountain switchbacks, I originally thought the Americans at the Games were just misguided. That is until we went riding on some long fast sweeping roads and they just walked away from me. That day I learned it was important to develop different techniques to be used on different road types.

Since then I think I've identified **four basic styles** which can be used to your advantage under different conditions.

The first is a **slalom style** which emphasizes the skateboard nature of a luge. You sit nearly upright and hold on to your handles. You keep your body mass fairly centered on the course and swing the board around obstacles underneath you. You can practice this style around cones, or even in and out of the dashed lines on a road. The technique comes in handy at slower speeds when aerodynamics aren't so critical. Use it to shift through sections with densely packed obstacles like landslide debris or a pack of crashing riders.

The second technique is useful for negotiating hard switchback turns. You can continue to call it the **German style** if you like; or feel free to call it the **switchback style**. This technique is similar to the way motorcycle road racers go through turns. Lean your body way off to the inside of the turn. It feels great and helps you better control the weight distribution during a slide. Because you're so far to the inside, it's much easier to control a luge that wants to highside. Also, by moving your body to the inside of the corner *before you start the turn*, less weight will be pivoting around and the wheels will hold a sharper line.

The third technique involves staying as aerodynamically tucked as possible. Useful on high speed, gradual turns, very little of your body loses direct contact with the luge. It's what you could call the **sweeper style**. Its emphasis is staying fast by staying tucked. Keep everything low and shift your head or hips to the side. Try to keep your feet on the pegs and use leg pressure to help steer the board. A luge optimized for this style will have a flatter (less leaned over) feel to it. Guys who like to compare street luge to car racing prefer this style.

The fourth style I'll identify as the **soaring style** since I already have 3 other S's going: Slalom, switchback, sweeper, and soaring . It's only applicable at the fastest speeds and I could have called it the **flying style**. No matter what terminology you use, at over 70 mph a luge can be controlled by aerodynamic input alone. It doesn't require lean turning. Keep the board balanced and open a palm to the wind. The resistance will pull you to that side. You will probably make minor lean shifts as well, as manipulating wind resistance won't get you through the harder turns. But once you learn to feel what the air is doing, even a subtle shift in your feet will move you from one side of the road to the other.

At these speeds you are *truly a luge "pilot."*

One of these riding styles is not superior to the others. Each is suited to a particular type of turn. High speed techniques won't get you around sharp corners and low speed techniques will be slower on a fast course. As you develop expertise in each style, you'll find yourself blending them together on the same run, and sometimes in the same turn. We don't ride only one kind of hill and courses contains different types of sections. Even though you prefer a particular style, develop a tool box of riding techniques and pull them out as the road demands.

Specialties

Practiced long enough, any sport can start to get dull. After hundreds of scuba dives, I began to take for granted even the most beautiful settings. One thing the scuba industry teaches is how to stay interested by branching into specialized areas of the sport.

I eventually took up shark divemastering, where you put yourself between the sharks and the divers scrambling into the shark cage. It's a specialty experience that keeps things fresh.

During one shark dive, after about two hours, I found my thoughts wandering. I realized "I'm underwater, pushing sharks away by hand—and I'm bored!"

It was not because the sport turned out to be less adventurous than anticipated. I had lost my ability to appreciate the wonder and danger of what was actually happening. That's when it becomes deadly. You may work to overcome your fear, but when you lose respect, it's time to get out.

Skydivers are still dying these days, but not because their parachutes don't open. To make their sport more interesting, many parachutists use critical, high speed canopies that crash into the ground and kill them if they don't land just right.

As you try out the following street luge specialities, use the experience to make yourself a better, more well rounded rider. If you feel the need to create your own to get one step further onto the edge (e.g. Blindfolded-naked-rocket-luge) then maybe it's time to switch sports.

Night Luge

Had I not grown up riding at night I would probably think it was adding an unnecessary risk to an otherwise manageable sport. Interestingly, many riders have actually learned this sport by street light. At the 1980 GMR race, Jim Ladd and Richard Marino took 1st and 3rd, listing their affiliation as NRRT (Night Riders Racing Team).

There are three big reasons to ride at night. First, many roads are practically deserted at night, so you are not competing with cars for a lane. Second, the cars on the road are less likely to surprise you as their headlights make them stand out more than during the day. Even coming around a corner, a car's lights precede it. The third reason is extended riding hours. If you go to work or school during the day, evening hours may be all that's left between weekends.

The obvious added dangers of riding at night involve **hitting something you didn't see,** or **being run over by someone who doesn't see you.** In both cases the answer is **lights.** Lots of lights. Don't leave home without them. Riding without adequate lights at night isn't more extreme, it's just plain stupid.

After a lot of riding at night, I think I have a hot set up. Get a powerful bicycle headlight with a wide angle beam. Mount it to the front of your luge. You can duct tape it to the luge between your feet. The purpose of this light is to provide general illumination so you can see where you are going. It will also allow any oncoming traffic to see you even better than they would during the day. The light won't tell them that you are a luge, but it will tell them you are something not to run over.

A single wide angle beam will provide a general view of what's in front, but attaching lights to your helmet will **let you look at things.** So in addition, I take two small flashlights and tape them to the top of my helmet. If I'm curious about something in the darkness, it lights right up when I turn my head to look at it. I can also use the beams to focus on the exact part of the road my wheels will roll over.

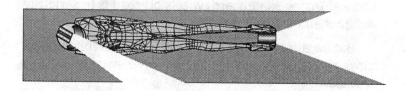

The last light I've found indispensable is a tail light. The red flashing kind that cyclists use are lightweight and inexpensive. You can stick them to the back of your helmet or your luge. Aside from looking totally cool as you pass someone, a flashing tail light tells motorists that you've given thought to safety.

Having a chase car behind you is even more important than it is during the day. However, don't be fooled into thinking you can use their headlights as a way to see the road. Your eyes will adapt to the additional brightness and when you get too far ahead of the car (which happens on a twisty road) you will plunge into darkness. Bring your own lights and let your eyes adapt.

The last tip is to never ride a road at night that you haven't thoroughly inspected during the day. A lot of times you'll be following the reflective dots down a black road and it will seem like a video game. What you may not see are potholes or other hazards that would be obvious on a day ride.

Dirt Luge

Off road vehicles of all types have large diameter wheels. The larger the wheel, the better it rolls over the cracks. Skateboard wheels, on the other hand, can be small because they were designed to roll over an artificially smooth surface. Taking skateboard wheels off road is to seriously violate their intended purpose.

But because we have surfing on water, on concrete, on snow, and now sky surfing; dirt was an inevitable niche to be filled.

Rick Wilson of XTreme-Wheelz markets the only skateboard wheels I know of actually intended for dirt. His XT-Wheelz™ are about 110 mm tall with tread made of rubber. And if there's dirt skateboarding, then I had to try dirt luge.

Off road vehicles tend to share two major features: Good ground clearance and good suspension. Street luge boards are designed with neither. So leave the dropped sled at home and put together a flat board with an extra set of riser pads under the trucks. You'll need the clearance or the larger wheels will rub the bottom of the board (or your legs). And use your heaviest duty trucks. This ain't no city ride.

Suspension is a big problem, so unless you want to outfit a rigid metal rail with springs, a flexible plywood board is the best cushioning you can hope for. And keep this in mind—dirt skateboards do have shocks—the rider's legs. On a luge, however, all impact goes straight into your butt and back . The XT-Wheelz make the ride more comfortable, and dirt has more give than pavement. Nevertheless, pick a smooth and well groomed trail.

Since I've made such a good case for the cross purposes of dirt and street luge, why even bother? Well, it's easier to find a hill with no traffic and you don't have to worry about stop signs. Police cars will probably be nonexistent (but so will your ride back up the hill).

Dirt tracks can have more interesting turns and undulations than roads designed for cars. And dirt riding is a whole new challenge. The main thrill is **sliding**. You can "pitch it out" in dirt luge like you can in dirt biking. There will be turns you attempt over and over again, just trying to get around without sliding out. It's fun. Plus all the flying dust makes you look like a rocket ship from hell.

Stopping requires a slight equipment change. The tire treads that grip the asphalt will just slide along a dirt trail. So bring hiking boots. Also, trade out the road race equipment for motocross pads and gloves. Abrasion drops down on the list of potential injuries in the dirt while sprains and contusions climb up.

Dirt can be fun because it's less controlled than streets are. But that also means a dirt path can be surprisingly more dangerous. All of the cautionary advice for street luge goes double when you ride a luge through dirt.

Rain Luge

OK. Rain luge is nutty. You'll get soaked, wreck your bearings, ruin your leathers, and you won't be able to stop worth a damn. But it *is* fun.

In a heavy downpour you won't be able to see and you'll most certainly crash. A light mist is better. Actually, what you really want is wet streets without any rain. But you'll still get soaked and filthy from all the crap your wheels throw up.

Aside from reduced visibility and seriously impaired braking, your board won't hold a turn and you'll slide all over. Which is exactly the point of rain luge—**sliding!** The road becomes one giant skid pad and you can learn the finer points of sliding at an accelerated pace. Count on sliding out, and sliding off your board. It's time to bring out the pads and welding gloves.

Staying warm is another obstacle. You're wet and have a lot of wind blowing on you. Recently, I've taken to wearing a very thin wet suit underneath an old set of leathers. Veteran racer Bob Ozman used to make a water proof barrier by taping trash bags to his body underneath his riding outfit. So there you have the high and low end of street luge rain gear. Consider what is available in between.

Rainy conditions also mean your face shield will fog up quickly. It seems to happen as soon as you get going about 40 mph. Suddenly you find, "Wow, this is slippery. Hey, I can't see a thing!" Make sure you can get your shield open quickly if this happens. To prevent fogging, prepare your face shield with an anti-fog treatment ahead of time. Put the shield down *before* you start rolling to test how badly it will fog. And put your helmet on early. It will help it warm to your temperature and keep rain drops from falling on your head.

Normal wheels can be very slippery over wet pavement. Some guys like to cut thin grooves into a set of wheels they save for rainy conditions. It's supposed to improve traction. Preparing wheels on a lathe will yield u n i f o r m results

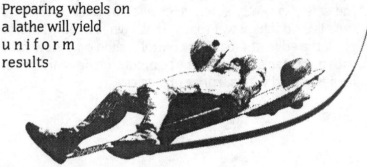

but I've also heard of guys who made grooves by pressing a screwdriver against their wheels as they rode. Depending on the road, forcing pointy things into your wheels seems like a good way to stab yourself. But it does get you thinking about creative ways to make rain wheels.

I have never grooved any wheels myself, but I did experiment with XT-Wheelz in the rain. They have tread like a tractor so they don't hydroplane as much as smooth wheels do. Even through puddles I found them to be very controllable. I had to make adjustments to fit them under my board, but the larger diameter helped when I ran over junk spilling out of the rain washed gutter.

Gerek Maddox (aka "Robo-luge") is the mad scientist of our sport. So I wasn't surprised to find he was also experimenting with XT-Wheelz under slippery conditions. But his roads get covered with snow and ice. After the plows came through, Gerek discovered the wheels allowed him to steer through the turns. But he couldn't slow down until he got to the bottom of the hill. Unless he crashed into the snowbanks lining the road.

Streets that are dull on a sunny day can be a blast when they are slicked down. A road without obstacles or traffic is most important. You can't stop very well and neither can the cars. I'm pretty sure I've crashed at least once every time I've ridden on wet roads. That's why I'm out there, to push the edge. If I learn to control a slide on a slow road with no obstacles then maybe I can control the board better on a fast road with surprise obstacles.

Endurance Luge

Most sports keep track of endurance records or have endurance events. Our sport could fit right in.

At first I thought it would be cool to establish a "Most Miles in 24 Hours" type record. Obviously, the higher the average speed, the more miles the rider can achieve. But then I realized that for every mile down hill there is car bringing you back to the top. So half of it becomes a car race, which is not at all to the point of what we do.

You could try to subtract driving time, but then someone could find a short, steep hill and take their time driving back up. They'd rest in the limo taking them uphill at 2 mph, and it's no longer an endurance event.

You could make it more interesting by not allowing the rider to go down the same section of road more than once. Then it would largely become a question of logistics and finding areas that had a lot of long, fast hills close together. You could always duplicate someone else's path and beat them by driving faster, but the beneficial part would be finding out the best parts of the country (or world!) to ride. So this idea has merit.

But I think the intent is really to have an event which is fun and tests the durability of riders and their equipment. One rule would be that the equipment you start with is what you stay on until you finish, get dropped, or quit. You can't change, adjust, or lubricate equipment. Your wheels and bearings must last the entire event.

Next is to set a fixed milestone distance and take all of the riders who want to participate. Bicyclists pick 100 miles as a significant distance. It's called a "Century" and the point is just to make the distance. It's probably a good milestone for street luge also. A hill which had an average downhill speed of 60 mph would be a "ripping" hill. You would need a fairly long hill so the starts, stops, and transitions didn't kill your average speed. Let's assume a 5 mile hill with close to a 70 mph top speed and a fast transport vehicle to bring you back up. That means 20 runs down and 20 back up the hill. 200 miles total distance for 200 minutes (or 3 hours, 20 minutes). Riders would eat on the way up the hill. You might schedule a 15 minute break every 25 miles which puts you around 4 hours for the event. Slower, shorter hills are probably more reasonable and extend that time estimate, as does more reasonable speed limit for a transport vehicle.

This also assumes a highly efficient event on the right hill with the right riders and drivers. My point is to justify a 100 mile distance (versus 10 or 1,000). The event would also have to establish a reasonable cut off for the riders. Something like "any rider not completing the 5 miles in 6 minutes is dropped from the event." Lose a wheel or bearing and you're out. If you wanted to pee before break time, you'd have to be extra fast.

As the sport exists today, riders would be challenged to make a Century. Their wheels probably wouldn't last. But wheels will get better and someone will find smoother, easier roads, so Centuries will get reputations for how tough they are. A "Freeway Century" would be a beginner run compared to the "GMR Century." As the courses got more technical, completing a Century on them would carry higher prestige. I can imagine collecting patches from the top 10 challenging rides and wearing them on my leathers.

And for those who found the 100 mile mark increasingly simple, there is always the cyclist model of the "Double Century" or even the dreaded "Quad."

Promoters would just have to be careful that the fatigue riders face on the longest rides didn't pose it's own unreasonable hazard.

Video Luge

A lot of things are fun to do, but don't translate well onto TV. Home movies are a prime example. A great vacation is fun to participate in, but don't ask the neighbors to watch the recap. Street luge is the opposite.

Tape a video camera to your lap and take a run at 50 mph. Because the perspective is so low, watching a playback makes it look like you're really hauling. Which is what it feels like. The good news about the X Games and other Broadcast coverage is TV has barely scratched the surface of what we really do. Someday there will be the "On Any Sunday" documentary version of our sport. Until then, home video is the best way to let your friends know what it's like.

Another good reason to tape your runs is that you can go back and memorize the road from the comfort of your living room. Sure, it's more fun to actually ride, but some hills don't lend themselves to frequent runs. If you find later that there will be a race on that hill, you can study the road without risking the race permit by taking unauthorized runs the month before.

I've hand carried my camera, which is risky if the run is the least bit challenging. Consequently, I've done most of my video work with a flat camera taped to my pelvis which gives a great perspective. Unfortunately, the shot gets occluded when I raise a leg for cornering and I can't ride full out. A camera helmet would be the most convenient, but I haven't splurged yet.

A tip I paid for the hard way is to buy and use an inexpensive clear filter. Don't think of it so much as a filter, but as a sacrificial lens. Even roads that seem really clean throw debris into your camera. And your best shots will be of other riders right in front of you. I never noticed how many little rocks get tossed up by our wheels until they were chipping my expensive video lens.

Racing

I've spent a lot of time mentioning racing, although the focus of this book is really more on recreational riding. You could (and someone will) dedicate an entire book to street luge racing tactics and techniques. For the purpose of this book, however, I categorize Racing as a street luge specialty activity.

When I first took up the sport, attending a race was really just a good way to get in more fun rides. You could pay a little money and someone had a truck to haul everyone back up the hill. Plus you got to meet a bunch of new guys who were into the same thing. Most of my actual luge time in the early '80s was spent just riding with friends. We were less concerned with being the first one down the hill and more concerned with looking good for the video camera.

These days, most of my riding is done at official races. The streets are blocked to other traffic and the major hazards are marked or protected by hay bales. Medical personnel are on hand in case there is an accident. Riding at a race is much safer than riding on open roads.

But **Street Luge Racing is dangerous!** This isn't contradictory to my initial description of our manageable sport. It's *racing* that's dangerous. You have to remember that the purpose of racing is to test the limits of the riders and their equipment. Often the winner is determined by who can brake the latest and hold the tightest turn. And since not everyone can hold the tightest turn, some will slide out and perhaps take other racers with them. And some of these racers will get hurt. Not always. But sometimes.

If you race aggressively, you will eventually end up in the situation where you get taken out by another racer, or lose control and take someone else out. God help you if you close out another racer's line to block his pass, and he is forced to crash. Someone who was your friend in the morning could end up crippled for life because you wanted a medal too badly.

But even with the risks, I love racing. Flying into a wickedly fast turn with three other pilots, everyone holding a line and watching out for the racer next to them, is a fabulous high. One that comes from balancing risky activity against trust in a fellow human being. The bonds formed between street luge racers are as strong as to the blood we hope will never spill.

Play Races

If riding at a permitted event is safer than riding on open streets, yet racing at a permitted event is dangerous by definition, how safe can racing on open streets be? Not very safe at all.

Most of the horrendous accidents in the sport have occurred on open roads, and usually when racers are practicing. You are still pushing the limits of your equipment, but there are cars or other hazards waiting when you blow a turn. Your concentration is split between the road and the other riders when it should be focused solely on the road. And emergency medical treatment may be hours away when someone does go in.

I have no hope that racers won't practice on open streets. The only way that will happen is when we can race every weekend at a permitted event, develop our skills there, and not need practice time between.

I would like to point out just a couple of things about play racing on open roads. First, at permitted races you get solo practice runs down the course. This means going slowly down the hill to help you learn the turns and braking points. Eventually, practice leads to qualifying, which is also solo. By the time you are actually racing against other riders, you should know the hill and can concentrate on where everyone else is riding next to you.

Contrast this to many "practice" sessions that occur on open roads. Everyone piles out of the truck like a pack of wild dogs. Testosterone is so thick it starts fogging the face shields. Guys who don't win official races have a new chance to prove they're fast. Previous champions have reputations to defend. No one wants to be "a pussy." Ultimately, everyone takes all the runs way too fast and leave little margin for error. Occasionally someone goes to the hospital.

When you ride open roads, do just that—RIDE them. If you find yourself out in front; slow down. The guys with whom you are riding may know the road better than you. They may have slowed for a reason. Plus, getting to watch other riders from behind is much more educational than watching your shoelaces dance in the wind.

Rider Collisions

Whether you are racing at a permitted event, or play racing on an open road, there are some special dangers involving the other riders. I could probably list forty, but there are two specific circumstances which seem to cause racing accidents over and over.

The first type of accident occurs when two equally fast racers have two different approaches to a single turn. Some racers want to take a turn from the inside and let the speed carry them back out. Other racers want to start the turn from the outside and clip the inside corner. Both are valid lines. The problem is when they intersect.

In diagram A, the white racer chooses to brake late and take the outside line. The grey racer is taking the shorter inside line and must swing wide exiting the turn. When the two riders meet up at (4), the grey racer is unable to avoid intersecting the white racer's line, and instead locks up with white's rear end. In white's opinion, grey crashed into the side of him. Grey's view is that he is already holding as tight

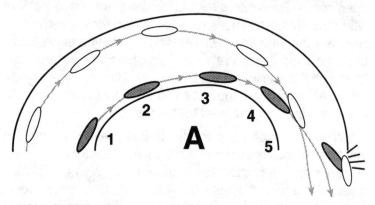

a line as possible and white cut him off. Actually, only white can prevent the accident by going wide with grey or waiting and diving in under him. Regardless of blame, once they make contact, neither rider can correct the line and both crash.

The second type of collision involves the greatest amount of controversy because the riders are close and both think the other should yield. Racing organizations try to make "right of way" rules, but the truth is if racers are overlapped and start to push on one another, both will crash.

In scenario (B), white attempts to move inside before fully completing the pass on grey. White prematurely assumes that since he can no longer see grey (2), he must be past. Instead, as white moves in, grey cannot go further inside and loses his front end against white's rear (3). Once they make contact, both riders go out of control (4). White cannot escape sliding into the opposite side of the track and grey is stuck with his front end pushing white to the outside (5). Spectator analysis might say that grey should've braked. However, the time elapsed between the good drafting position at (2) to the lock up at (3) happens before anyone could get on the brakes. Ultimately, white needs to respect grey's commitment to the inside line.

Both of the illustrated scenarios involve the trailing inside rider taking out the rear end of the leading rider. I concentrated on these examples as most other scenarios are recoverable by heads-up racers. The easy lesson is to leave room for a racer trapped on the inside. You may believe you are preventing an inside pass, but you are really either creating an excellent draft for a racer you have just passed, or are about to have your rear end taken out in the impending two man crash.

Generic Racing Rules

I was originally going to lay out a grid comparing racing rules from various organizations. After compiling my materials, however, I realized that they were all much more alike than not. Also, minor changes over the last few years suggest that the various rule sets will continue to converge in the future.

Be aware, however, that a minor technical issue can keep you out of a race. Always get a copy of the rules an event organizer plans to use. There is also no reason why big shifts in the sport couldn't significantly alter the rules listed on the following page.

As a consultant on Street Luge Racing, I have a few principles from which I believe all racing rules should stem:

1. Promote growth of the sport.

   Bad rules will drive people away, and rules that drive people away are bad. Rules should encourage competitive manufacturing and event promoter involvement. Rules should allow technological advances in the sport.

2. Promote safety

   The drive to win will naturally cause people to become more reckless. This must be counterbalanced by rules.

3. Preserve the integrity of the sport.

   Rider enclosures, non-lean steering, or motors, would turn Street Luge into a different sport.

4. Ensure fair competition

   This includes objective scoring, non-preference for a particular manufacture's equipment, and ensuring that unsponsored riders have a chance to win.

5. Rules which benefit the rule makers should be avoided.

Basic Rule Set used by most organizations

Safety Equipment:

Full leathers.

Full face DOT approved helmet w/shield.

Full fingered leather gloves.

Adequate foot and ankle protection.

Luge Specs:

Lean steer only.

No rider enclosures. Aerodynamic devices limited by individual organization.

No mechanical brakes, nor anything that interferes with the feet being used for stopping.

No dangerous obstacles between rider's legs (e.g. handlebars).

No sharp or hard surfaces which present a danger to other riders.

Truck width limited to 12". Type may be limited, *Depending On Organization (DOO)*.

Wheels 70 mm - 127 mm (5") DOO.

Skateboard or in-line skate type bearings.

Hardware mounted with grade 8 bolts and nylock nuts.

Construction materials subject to approval by individual organization.

8.5' - 10' max length, DOO.

Max width either 22", 2" wider than rider, or no wider than rider, DOO.

Max weight 40 - 50 lbs, DOO.

Bumper, nerf bar, and foot peg specs DOO.

Number plate DOO

Racing Organizations

The discussion of racing organizations is necessarily one of history. As promoters gain and lose interest, so does the visibility of their organizations. Check the Internet to see who is holding races. New organizations will come up, promoters get tired and drop out, and people come out of retirement.

Signal Hill

Not so much an organization as a series of races from 1975 - 78 hosted by the U.S. Skateboard Association. Signal Hill is short, steep and straight. The plan was to have high speed skateboard races which polarized between regular stand-up boards and head first enclosed skatecars. The winners did product endorsements, and the races were covered by *SkateBoarder* and *Sports Illustrated.*

Unfortunately because of the mounting participant and spectator injuries, the event was subsequently cancelled. The skateboarding industry abandoned speed runs as a once "curious facet of competitive skateboarding."

Roger Hickey was the only participant to have continued from Signal Hill into modern street luge competition, bringing its influence with him. While racing his skate car, Roger met Sam Puccio, whom *SkateBoarder* magazine described as the "defending champion...again impressive with his design of simplistic 2"x4" construction and his luge style technique."

Even with no formal advertising, the 1977 Signal Hill Speed Run had a top prize of $1,000, over 4,000 spectators and speeds just under 60 mph.

URA (Underground Racers Association)

After Signal Hill, Roger Hickey, Beau Brown, Rick Denton, and Don Baumea, formed the URA which held non-insured, non-permitted events.

To my knowledge, this was the first organization to hold a true street luge type event. I attended one of the early meetings and voiced a concern that "Underground Racers" would never get city permits for a race. I suggested trying a different name. I was not invited back.

The URA would hardly be a foot note except the series culminated in the historic 1980 Glendora Mountain Road (GMR) race which made the cover of *SkateBoarder* magazine.

The URA carried over some of the Signal Hill limitations such as 12" axles and 5" wheels. They also introduced some defining features such as no mechanical brakes, and no rider enclosures. Roger even had an aluminum board made of an upside down motorcycle ramp.

Of the original 1980 GMR competitors, Bob Ozman, Marcus Rietema, and myself have raced in the X Games. I would hardly be surprised if a few other veterans came out of retirement to race again.

In 1990, Roger organized a 10 year anniversary race at GMR, this time securing sponsorship and permits. Alec Schroeder covered the event for *Poweredge Skateboard Magazine* and raced as a first timer, taking a very close 2nd in the amateur class.

Alec continued with the sport and went on to become the number one qualifier in the '95 X Games. Roger, on the other hand, broke his arm during practice, leaving the door open for Ken Kinnee to win the pro division, followed by future X Games medalists Shawn Goulart and Lee Dansie.

LLIRA (Land Luge International Racing Assn.)

Ken Kinnee and Bob Pereyra formed their own "Max Racing" team and attracted quite a bit of media attention in the early '90s. Ken worked on forming an official sanctioning body for the sport and played around with calling it the International Land Luge Association (ILLA) and in August of 1990 announced the Land Luge International Racing Association (LLIRA).

LLIRA never actually put on any racing events, but it did produce a newsletter and a fairly comprehensive rule book. It also set the ground work for the formation of ILRRA and RAIL.

ILRRA (International Luge Road Racing Assn.)

Ron Amos and Bob Pereyra continued the quest for a formal racing organization, forming the ILRRA. Newsletters, a rule book, membership, and patches marked a new era in visual professionalism for the sport.

In 1991, ILRRA sent invitations to a filming for the television show "the extreme EDGE." It wasn't a racing event, but was noteworthy because of the large number of top riders involved. In 1993, ILRRA put on it's first and only competition, piggybacking on the Monterey Camel GT auto race at Laguna Seca.

RAIL (Road Racers Assn. for Intl. Luge)

After the '93 Laguna Seca race, Bob Pereyra put out the first RAIL newsletter. He announced a perceived conflict of interest between Ron's UFO Sports and a rider based organization.

RAIL put on a '94 Laguna Seca race and organized the first ESPN Extreme Games competition in 1995. The RAIL

"Road to the Games" series commenced, leading to the retitled '96 ESPN X Games.

Even with a different event organizer for the '97 and '98 X Games, RAIL continues to put on excellent races and the RAIL series top finishers have guaranteed invitations to the games.

RAIL draws considerable positive attention to the sport and has gone on to become the oldest continually operating luge racing organization.

RAIL, Inc.
18734 Kenya Street
Northridge, CA 91326
818-368-6826

FIGR (Federation of Intl. Gravity Racing)

Roger Hickey formed his own racing organization which featured his special GF1 Gravity Cars, Speedboarding, and in 1994, a regular Street Luge series. The races were characterized by creative format changes including dual slalom and the first official night race.

In 1995, the number of luge racers expanded to allow a separate amateur class series. Ron Amos made these FIGR races his home turf, and introduced new riders on his UFO team; racers like Mike Colabella, Tom Mason, and Biker Sherlock.

Roger shouldered the financial burden for the races but had behind the scenes help from many people including Marcus Rietema and Perry Fisser. When Roger put FIGR in moth balls, both men took that experience and went on to carry the torch.

EDI (Extreme Downhill International)

Perry and Laurie Fisser formed EDI to keep the original FIGR racers together. During a year of great personal and financial sacrifice, the Fissers worked hard to create an atmosphere of street luge racing as a family event.

The races leading up to the final were all held at Bonelli Park in San Dimas, California. The hill was short (.4 miles) and the speeds weren't much above 50 mph. But with repeated controlled conditions, the racers had good opportunity to experiment with the technical side, visit with friends, and get new riders involved with the sport.

In contrast to the tame nature of Bonelli Park, the EDI National Championship race was held on Tuscany Hill in Lake Elsinore California. Speeds were over 70 mph (without even starting at the top of the hill!).

During the first six bimonthly events, EDI had 14 GF1 racers, 28 Speedboarders, 28 Luge Experts, and 49 Sport Luge competitors. Many racers at the top today have Perry and Laurie to thank for keeping them involved.

At the last event in '96, Mike Sherlock (Biker's Dad) announced he had bought EDI from Perry and Laurie and that Biker and Brad Strandlund would join the Fissers in running the organization.

After the finals in '97, the Fissers announced their retirement from organizing (but NOT racing) and Biker announced his plans for redirecting the organization toward a televised international pro series. Like RAIL, for '97 and '98, the top 5 EDI series finishers have guaranteed invitations to the X Games.

Extreme Downhill International
1666 Garnet Ave. #308
San Diego, CA 92109
619-272-3095

IGSA (International Gravity Sports Association)

In 1996 Marcus Rietema hosted a series of meetings attended by racers wanting to come up with a National Point Series and rules which would be acceptable to all organizations. Not everyone came to terms on what was to be accomplished, but eventually a core group began to meet weekly. For months they pursued forming a member based nonprofit corporation and solicited input from other riders.

The meetings went on hold during the '96 X Games season. In the beginning of '97, Shawn Goulart introduced Marcus to the ESPN directors. Consequently, Marcus was awarded the '97 X Games contract and held an Open Qualifying race under the IGSA banner. The first qualifier resulted in 28 slots to the X Games thanks to the volunteer efforts of Bob Ozman, Ted Schroeder, Alec Schroeder, and myself.

The '97 X Games were well organized and Marcus drew the '98 contact with an option for future years. Marcus has a series of events planned and IGSA has 5 series slots for the '98 X Games along with 15 Open Qualifier slots.

IGSA
638 N. Crestview Drive
Glendora, CA, 91741
626-963-5304

RAIL East

Michael Shannon was instrumental in the professional appearance of the RAIL rule book and materials. Living back East and continually flying out for West Coast races, Michael realized a need to hold races that were more local to the aspiring East Cost racers. Starting in 1997, RAIL East has held dual events with RAIL, along with its own unique RAIL East events.

So far, the RAIL East events have featured some of the most epic hills since the GMR days. Michael coordinated an Ansted, West Virginia race which directly follows the annual Bridge Day jump from the New River Gorge Bridge. The locals were so excited to have a street luge follow-up, they paved a narrow twisty road featuring a 60 mph straight followed by a hard 90° right, 50 yards before the finish line!

Another race put on by Michael was "Sam's Gap" which was over 4 miles long and featured a 12 man format! Whether RAIL East continues as an extension of RAIL, or becomes its own race series, each event is certainly worth attending.

RAIL East
143 Sycamore Dr.
Arden, NC, 28704
704-254-4592

Hot Heels

Working in Germany as a snowboard instructor, Stefan Wagner decided it was "so sad to go down the road by car" after work each day. So in 1989 he and Ralph Kohler started butt boarding the 27 km Kaunertal Glacier Road. No foot rests, no hand holds—just 4 foot boards sliding through 17 miles of switchbacks. In 1992, the Germans made it official, forming the Hot Heels organization which holds an annual race down the mountain road.

Attempting to preserve the spirit of the early runs, Hot Heels limits board lengths to 120 cm (4 feet) with 5 kilograms (11 lbs.) max weight. Nevertheless, top speeds still reach over 60 mph down the challenging course! After struggling with weather conditions and the high cost of hay bales, in 1995 the track was shortened to a more hospitable section at the bottom of the mountain.

Competitions are held in four or six man elimination formats with fields ranging between 21 to 35 athletes. The racers come mainly from Germany, but the Austrian, Swiss, and French are also represented. In 1993, John Kaye was the first American to try the course, but finding the turns too difficult he chose not to compete. Starting in 1998, Hot Heels is creating an Open Class, hoping to encourage more international racers to come over with their standard competition luges.

The Hot Heels racers have been tough X Games competitors taking home a disproportionately large amount of prize money and medals.

Hot Heels e.V, c/o Frank Vogelsang
Kruppstr. 11
d-10559 Berlin, Germany

Sssprint (Street Sled Sport Racers Intl.)

While competing as bungee jumpers in the 1995 Extreme Games, members of the Oxford Stunt Factory got their first close look at street luge. Ding Boston returned home to England and convinced his fellow impoverished students that street luge was an easy and affordable sport. One they had to try.

Midnight drops through local streets quickly evolved into a racing organization with closed tracks and regular competitions. Sssprint's racing season runs September to September, corresponding with the college academic year.

With about 10 hard-core British competitors, Sssprint holds open races and has begun to draw participants from the general population. Aluminum rails outfitted with Z-Rollers and Labeda 90 mm wheels are common. Members also bring extra gear and boards to accommodate the half dozen or so new adventurers that show up.

Courses are about 1/2 to 1 mile long and top speeds average 50 mph. Tracks are narrow, very twisty, and often wet. Competitions are based on time trial runs, with course records established and tracked on Sssprint's web site (hosted by Guy Coates).

Occasionally racers will run the hill 2 or 3 at a time with spectacular wipe outs onto the grassy borders. Ding still appears to be the Brit to beat although several other racers are nipping at his heels. Luge is beginning to gain attention throughout the UK with the BBC running a feature on "They Who Dare."

Given the consistency of their racing involvement, the British racers were conspicuously absent from the '95 – '97 X Games. However, through his internet contacts, top Sssprint racer John Maher is making sure that the UK is properly represented in '98. John has also been instrumental in organizing the first "European tour." The plan is for top U.S. racers to compete in the May Sssprint Race and then travel with the Brits to Austria where Allied forces take on the best of Hot Heels.

Sssprint
33a Canal Street
Oxford, OX2 6BQ
Tel 01865 311179

Checking The Web

Because of the highly dynamic nature of this sport and its organizations, only the Internet can seem to keep pace. Race schedules and results are being posted on the web even sooner than they are mailed to the competitors. On the other hand, some sites perpetuate misinformation or lie fallow for months.

An easy URL to remember is John Lewis' **www.StreetLuge.com**. Most sites are cross linked, so you'll be able to find your way to "Land Luge Las Vegas," "Dr-GoFast," "EPIC," "Panic Street Luge," "Sssprint" and other great resources.

Gravity Car racer Martyn Evans worked with Marcus Rietema to put up **www.IGSA.com**. It includes dates on IGSA events and a downloadable version of the latest IGSA rulebook. If you are hoping to go the X Games while it's under the IGSA banner, you should check out this site.

Michael Shannon's **www.RoadLuge.org** was a hit the first week it was announced. It is beautifully designed and includes discussion sections on racing rules and designs. Michael has been dedicated to the sport for a long time and works for a company that designs web sites. You can expect RoadLuge.org to become a continual source of important information.

Even if all of the above sites went out of commission (not likely), somewhere the Internet will have current information on the sport. If you type "Street Luge" into a search engine, you should find the latest sites with up-to-date addresses, phone numbers, products, and events.

Old School Ethics

The press after the '96 X Games brought attention to something identified as "The New School." Biker Sherlock, Tom Mason, and Mike Colabella were really it's only visible members and even poor "Coli" had been dragged along.

The New School engaged in Combat Luge with the motto "When in doubt—take 'em out!" It was a notion so foreign to any of the established luge racers that the sport had no rules to adequately prevent such behavior.

Mason was the most identified and vocal of the camp. "It's racing . . . in racing the [only] object is to win." The New Schoolers used examples from dirty car racing or dirt bike tactics to justify their ethic. But after only one year, there were no more members of the New School philosophy. They all grew up.

Normally, new racers can't rise to notoriety without having to learn the ethic of their sport first. Champions dictate the standards of behavior, and the new guys watch and learn from the pros. Normally.

However, these were particularly talented riders, racing short courses which necessitated a fast start. Experienced racers weren't prepared for the impact the push start would have. Historically, they might have lagged the start on purpose, drafting and passing throughout a longer course. It was a new twist that made a quick rise to stardom possible. And with the public attention came a false notion of our championship values.

Street luging with your friends is an enjoyable and manageable activity. Even friendly bumping and pushing can be fun and relatively safe. Racing adds a degree of aggression and hence danger. Combat luge is insanely dangerous. It would be like competitive skydiving where you wrestle your opponent and try to stop each other from opening the chute. It's just retarded.

Had it not received attention from *Rolling Stone* magazine, the whole New School issue would have been forgotten. But new riders hear about it and decide not to race or come ready to fight. The truth is, **there is no "New School." There are only new riders who have yet to learn the necessary ethic of the sport.**

During the qualifying runs at the '97 X Games, Bret Bachelor suffered a horrendous injury, rolling about, clutching a flopping leg. The racers watched his agony back on the pit side monitors. "You know what's the BEST thing about Bret snapping his leg in half?" I pointedly asked in Tom's direction, "No one else forced him into the hay bales." It was already a moot point, as Tom had been sickened by the injuries witnessed a year earlier. The so called "New School" racers were perfect gentlemen for the entire '97 season. And they were faster than ever.

"I think we brought out the physical nature of the sport," says Biker, "but we never intentionally hurt anyone. Combat Luge was a creation of the media." Biker went on to run EDI and became intolerant of any dangerous behavior. It didn't take long to learn the difference between close quarters racing and taking someone out. None of us feel winning is worth crippling someone we race against. The enemy should be the course itself.

The true essence of this sport is a cooperative venture between close riders and a hazardous run. The ultimate measure of a rider is not how quickly he can get down the hill, but how many veterans feel comfortable drifting a hard turn next to him.

Learn your skills thoroughly. Being fast at the expense of your racing companions doesn't mean a thing. The experienced riders could kill you in a second. But that's not what they're about.

The Future

The Future is often associated with advanced materials. When skateboarding moved from metal to urethane wheels, the performance gains were incredible. The obvious next step was to improve on the crude wooden decks. Almost every guy I knew built or bought a plexiglass board because in the '70s that *really* looked like the future. I also had a plastic *Jaws* board, and tried some cool fiberglass and aluminum decks. But twenty years later, the future turned out to be laminated wood.

If skateboarding ever reached a "high-tech" zenith, it was in the late '70s at Signal Hill. They had sophisticated trucks, large custom wheels, and wind tunnel designs. But after too many crashes, the industry turned its back on downhill skateboarding and we dropped into the Dark Ages. Street luge has been a way of picking up those pieces and moving on.

Pushing for faster speeds and fewer accidents has meant looking at the skateboard in entirely new ways. Individuals who loved adventure, innovation, and creativity kept the sport alive, even when the rest of the world stopped looking. Street luge does not exist because ESPN created a name and turned on the cameras. The cameras were on because something already existed. Something really cool.

Massive exposure means that things are picking up fast. When I started this book, it was difficult to get 70 mm wheels. Now manufactures are selling larger wheels designed for the sport. We have trucks designed specifically for racing. **We are entering a renaissance.**

So where do we go from here? The key is in the plural nature of "we." No single person can possibly grow this sport to its potential. It will take a cooperative effort of manufactures, racers, promoters, and retailers to satisfy the enormous demand. We need to move from a participation base of 200 to 2,000, and plan on servicing 20,000 in the next ten years. And no one will do it alone.

A big part of growing the sport is making it accessible to as many people as possible. Once upon a time, scuba diving was reserved for the macho elite. You had to build your own gear which performed poorly and the places where you could dive were limited. Sound familiar?

I can envision a future with much more aerodynamic boards. They are inexpensive because they are made of a durable plastic. Or they may be made of some future composite. Or maybe aluminum. Or fiberglass. Or wood.

A future where we are not considered any more extreme than skiing, but are much more popular. And what we trade off in exclusivity we will gain in high performance equipment and courses designed to challenge the best of our current abilities. Some things will be lost and new things will replace them. The panic of running from the cops will be replaced by the thrill of trying to get through a roller-coaster course with high banked turns, jumps, and corkscrew loops.

And along the way, some of us will get famous, and some of us rich. And some will get hurt instead. And new people will come into the sport with unheard of talents. And fantastic ideas. And we will all make this future together.

Luge Parks

If there were no ski resorts, there would be today no more skiers than there are lugers. For our sport to move from an "extreme sport novelty" to a major recreation like skiing, we need a better place to practice than on the city streets.

If no one wanted to pony up for a dedicated park, they could make use of an off-season ski resort. It wouldn't be ideal like a year round park would be, and freezing plays hell on the condition of paved roads. But as the access roads and chair lifts are already in place, a ski resort operator may see the opportunity. Eventually though, the luge experience at a purpose built park would lure away the best participants.

A dedicated luge park would require buying or leasing an undeveloped hill and paving runs. Since we're not running heavy vehicles, the courses should be no more expensive than a series of bike paths to construct. The way back up the hill could be by motor vehicle, or even an old tow rope adapted from a ski resort. To enhance safety, wide rivers of sand would run down both sides of each path. The sand would be soft, prevent runaway boards, and be very easy to maintain. A pro shop at the top could sell equipment and, of course, replacement bearings for the "Sand Sharks." There would also be a place to sell the economically important snacks and sodas.

When visitors first registered at the park, they would have their picture digitized and be issued an electronic pass. The pass would identify them before entering each run, and keep track of charges and statistics. With today's technology, sensors could automatically display speeds and split times along the course and video cameras could automatically track the riders. Large screen displays could be set up for spectators, automatically informing them of each pilot's name, with insert photos and statistics. The riders themselves could take home a tape to show their families and study technique.

Careful layout of the paths could provide runs with varying degrees of difficulty while minimizing the amount of land needed. Courses can be terribly exciting without ever exceeding 50 mph and the type of purpose built street luge courses could far outpace anything designed for cars. Visitors to the park would have to prove themselves on the slower runs before moving on to the more challenging ones. Some paths could split and come back together. One side or the other could be blocked off creating a new rider experience with minimal additional pavement. Connector paths could allow even greater course variety.

Such a park would quickly become a natural for holding racing competitions. Since insurance and permits would already be secured, events could take place every weekend. After the first park proves successful, more parks will certainly follow, all across the country. And local experts would want to compete with experts from other parks; and eventually there would be regional competitions like there are in other national sports. There would be an ongoing series, and X Games champions would emerge from park clientele instead of from off the streets. There is just no way that public roads can provide the type of intense skill building that would occur at a well designed luge park.

Consistent runs with accurate timing means the newest and fastest equipment would be designed and tested at the parks. A well designed facility would include analytical instruments to test the performance of individual components, and even a mini wind tunnel!

It would be easy to have training boards, training leathers, and training helmets; and teach new people to ride on coned training runs. At first there would be part time instructors who taught only on weekends, and eventually a class of professional instructors would emerge. In turn, this would create a market for training materials and training tapes.

There are lot of people who see and read about this sport and would love to try it. However, they are unwilling to build their own boards and brave the local traffic. Particularly after they reach a certain level of maturity. But with this maturity comes earning power. And these same people would definitely pay for lessons from professional instructors, would pay for safe equipment, and would pay to practice every weekend. They already do it with skiing, scuba diving, and skydiving. Once this group discovers how amazing our sport really is, they won't be so willing to spend their money on being cold or wet again.

Guide Books and Paraphernalia

Although this is the first real book on Street Luge, I imagine there will be several more to come. Expect future editions of this book, so look at the front dates and see if it's time to "upgrade."

There is also a need for other supplementary books. An interesting "**Complete History of Street Luge**" could feature a lot of personal interviews along with historic photographs. Every person participating in this sport is an amazing individual. I'd certainly buy a book about them.

Then there is "**Winning Street Luge Techniques**" which would be ghost written for a recent X Games champ, and will supposedly give all the secrets of how to be aerodynamic, how to draft, how to pick the best line, etc.. It could even include "**10 Best Street Luge Training Exercises**" which would consist of various sit-up regimes, seated rowing and triceps pushdowns (to build muscles for fast starts).

Scuba diving, rock climbing, and cycling are all mature sports with guide books. The advantage of a guide book is that someone experienced has already scoped out the promising areas. A "**Street Luge Guide Book**" would include various roads in a region, their length, speed, and notable dangers. If demand warrants, regional books could pop up like "**Epic Luge Hills of Southern California**." A guide would also need to cover local laws, weather information, equipment, food, and the location of the nearest hospital.

A well planned and maintained web site could make some of these book ideas obsolete, but there is much more to producing a valuable resource than getting excited and putting up a few pages. I can see where something dynamic like a web site has incredible advantages over printed material. As we develop ways for authors to be well compensated for electronic material, we'll get sites that are even more valuable than books. In the meantime, don't plan on scanning in my book and putting it up on the web for free. Someday I may be drifting a super fast turn on the inside of you, and you'll want to be on really good terms with me then.

Log books are popular with scuba divers and skydivers. Essentially they are a way to document your experience level. Even though Roger Hickey started only a few years before I did, I'll bet he's ridden 20 times as many miles. Some of the new guys who ride several times a week could also quickly catch up. Experience isn't just how many years ago you started. It's the number and quality of miles. A breakdown of accumulated minutes spent above 70 mph coupled with total number of switchbacks taken at speed would be a quick measure of experience. Throw in the number of night and rain runs, and you can separate the men from the boys.

We don't have a dedicated magazine yet, because we don't have enough participants to warrant it. Someday we will. While we wait, we can aspire to a regular column in a multi-extreme sport format.

A video tape doesn't yet exist for our sport (that should *really* date this edition). I don't know why someone hasn't done a whole series of tapes, as photogenic as the sport is. We will need a tape of "**Epic Luge Runs**," "**Sliding Pilots of the Pavement**" and of course, "**Street Luge Crashes vol. 3**."

And what about a "**Street Luge Studs**" calendar? Actually, expect a "**Babes of Street Luge**" first. More women are entering this sport, and they're much more attractive!

A longtime dream of mine is a full length, Bruce Brown "On Any Sunday" type documentary. We need a similar visionary to communicate our truth. This sport has an unparalleled beauty and excitement, and the rest of the world deserves to see it as we do. Over the years, other riders have confessed similar secret desires, so we are on the inevitable path to such a film. I've always hoped I could be part of such a project, but I know it will eventually be accomplished.

Specialized Gear

Throughout the book I've really lamented that the sport isn't big enough for any dedicated Street Luge equipment companies. Actually there are a few racers and a few dedicated fans that are making equipment for the sport. As time goes on, more and more small companies are popping up, hoping to break into the pre-built luge board market. Many of these guys are racers who are learning to build things, and some are professional fabricators who are learning about luge.

Many of these companies are run out of people's garages and may not be in business by the time you read this. On the other hand, Hobie™ was once a guy making surfboards in his garage and now it's a multi-national corporation.

I include these listings, not as an advertisement for these products, nor as an endorsement. I don't use everything here and may not even agree with the manufacturer's design philosophy. I'm also not including all general resellers of equipment. Just people who have specific Street Luge equipment, in case you want to contact them and try their products. And to give thanks for their support and dedication.

Labeda Wheels

Labeda is a large wheel manufacturer with distributors across the country. I've included them here because you'll probably have to get your local skate shop to special order their Street Luge wheels. Just because it's not in the display case, doesn't mean it's not available.

XTreme Wheelz

You can buy XT-Wheelz at many skate shops, but Rick Wilson continues to add new products to his line. You might check with them directly to see what's new for Street and Dirt Luge.

12528 Kirkham Ct. #5
Poway, CA 92064
619-679-5599

Randal Speed Trucks

Randal is another manufacturer that is distributed through skate shops. If you can't find the latest in street luge trucks try them direct.

261 Riconada Ave
Palo Alto, CA 94301
650-327-5566
RandalDesign@earthlink.net

Moe Speed

A perfect example of a racer starting a business in his garage and growing from there. Aside from after market parts, there are also Moe Speed boards. Moe works closely with pro class racer Steve Fernando, so you know what they sell has been tested and works. Moe hasn't hit skate shop distribution yet, but does have a web presence and many loyal customers.

1006 N. Sunset Canyon Dr.
Burbank, CA 91504
818-843-8698

Bullet Board

Dean Salter and Jim Kiper are racers that make custom metal boards in their garage. But whether you rent commercial space or build at home, it's track performance that counts.

www.BulletBoard.com
626-918-7290

Sled Manufacturing

Aside from running a top notch racing organization, Bob Pereyra supplies complete boards and other racing equipment. He also is a great source for the special visors used on the Wedge helmets.

18734 Kenya Street
Northridge, CA 91326
818-368-6826

Dregs

When Biker Sherlock isn't piling up gold medals or running EDI, he also has a thriving skateboard and luge manufacturing business. Check with Dregs for supplies and complete boards, including Dr. GoFast luges and Speedboard equipment.

1666 Garnet Ave. #308
San Diego, CA 92109
619-272-3095
www.DregsSkateboards.com

Dr. GoFast

Jarret Ewanek is a degreed engineer who cut his teeth building the most technically advanced GF1 cars. He has a passion for Speedboarding and now he's turned his focus to luge design. As an active racer, Jarret engineers custom equipment and tries his more "creative" designs on himself first. He also specializes in carbon fiber applications.

1268 W. 134 Street
Gardena, CA 90247
310-715-6838
www.Dr-Gofast.com

Powerhouse Roadboards

Powerhouse is an example of an existing manufacturer that wanted to sell luge boards. Even though John King used 6061-T6 aluminum channel and built to the rules, he met resistance from the racing community. Consequently, John entered the '97 EDI Nationals and brought his boards with him. His basic rail design is professionally built and illustrates that you don't have to race to put something together well.

8545 Arjons Drive Suite P
San Diego, CA 92126
619-695-1430

X-team

Dino Nussbaum was a racer that experienced the difficulty of getting equipment first hand. Consequently, he started the first dedicated Street Luge shop. Dino will mail order anywhere in the country.

5224 Katherine st.
Simi, CA 93063
805-579-8326

Subterfuge Land Luge

The first internet luge store, Subterfuge was started almost as quickly as Tim Cayer and Travis Tripp got interested in racing. Aside from "on the road" training, they've learned a lot about street luge through email and the message boards. They even started their own website. Tim has a motorcycle shop and is applying his experience to the retail end of our sport.

272 N. Village Rd.
Loudon, NH 03301
1-800-484-7293 x3134
www.LandLuge.com

Incident Reports

One of my favorite parts of *Scuba Diver* magazine is "I Learned About Diving From That." This is a dedicated section where a hapless diver explains where he makes a big mistake and almost dies as a consequence. The benefit is to other divers who hopefully avoid repeating the mistake.

The FAA puts out accident reports on crashes for the benefit of the Airline industry. Likewise, *Parachutist* includes "Incident Reports" which describe fatalities in that sport. Some day, when street luge has enough participants to support a regular magazine, it will also need to publish periodic incident reports.

This is not typical of information for a book, but barring another source, I'll give you examples of street luge accidents of which I am aware, had permission to use, required hospital care, and occurred between 1994 and 1997. **There were no fatalities.**

I respect all of the riders included and consider "There but for the grace of God go I." Everyone who volunteered to be included knew their way down a hill and was using appropriate gear. They wanted you to know what's at risk, and hopefully provide some perspective on what to avoid. Try not to repeat their mistakes, but remember you are hardly immune.

Rider:

Zac Bernstein, 21 year old male

Experience Level:

Sport class racer for 1 year

Description:

After a weekend of organized racing, the rider joined four other racers for a fun ride down Glendora Mountain Road. The road was closed due to a landslide in the middle of a 9 mile section. The plan was to be dropped off by car at the top, ride the first section, walk around the washout, and continue the ride down to the car waiting below.

The first several miles went smoothly and the rider moved into the lead position although it was his first time on the road. As the pace picked up, and the turns became more challenging, the rider in second position slid out. Two turns later, the lead rider went too wide and ended up bouncing through the weeds covering the dirt shoulder. He had slowed to approximately 25 mph.

All riders stopped at this point to regroup for safety reasons. The lead rider, however, did not get up out of the weeds.

The other riders found he had crashed through wooden slats covering a narrow concrete storm drain. His entire board and body fit inside and were several feet below the level of the road. Blood was running from under his helmet onto his chest and he had an obvious deformation of his leg. After removing his helmet, he claimed he would be OK and needed a minute to catch his breath. He was coughing up small amounts of blood.

The members of the riding party were able to keep him on his board and lift him out of the storm drain. First aid was performed to stop any external bleeding. Given the location of the accident, the group decided it would take far too long to get a vehicle to the accident site. Duct tape was used to immobilize the rider's leg and he was placed in the lap of another rider. He rode tandem several more miles until the washout. The group used the board as a litter and carried him across, where once again he rode tandem to the car waiting at the bottom of the road.

Injury:

Lacerated throat (requiring stitches)

Dislocated collar bone

4 broken ribs

Collapsed lung

Broken ankle (Cast)

Broken wrist (Cast)

Broken hand (Cast)

Ball broken off femur (requiring surgery, pins, cast)

Analysis:

That the rider was going too fast on an unfamiliar road is evidenced by his failure to stay on the pavement. It seems even less excusable as he was leading at the time he should have been watching the more experienced riders for cues to road hazards.

However, he was not riding at a reckless pace, nor through a section that appeared to have hazards off the pavement. None of the other riders anticipated any danger when he went into the weeds.

The lesson is that going off the road, even at slower speeds can bring the rider in contact with unseen dangers. From inside a car, discarded fence stakes, broken glass, and rocks appear to be normal roadside debris. On a luge, they are hazardous and potentially deadly objects.

Recovery:

Zac spent one month in California and Utah hospitals, another month in physical therapy, and then two more months in casts. He had the casts removed early so that he could race a few weeks later!

Rider:

Rob Maushund, 31 year old male

Experience Level:

Pro class racer for 5 years. Previously raced for "Max Racing" and "Fluid Drive"

Description:

On the last day of a three day luge trip, the group followed a pickup truck down a now familiar run. A camera was pointed out the back of the truck, hoping to capture a high speed group run.

At about 40 mph, the lead rider began to overtake the truck. Instead of slowing or passing, he put both feet on the truck's bumper, hoping to provide a more interesting shot. The rider had successfully tried this stunt on several occasions before, but this time he lost balance and rolled off his luge.

While tumbling, one hand was trapped briefly between his body and the road which ground through his glove. As he rolled, the other hand was run over by a following rider. He stayed on the road and his protective gear held together.

Injury:

Severe abrasion to left hand requiring stitches

Broken right hand (Cast)

Analysis:

The rider had the requisite skill to pull off the impromptu stunt. Had it come off successfully, it would have been an amusing addition to an interesting videotape. Instead it provided interesting crash footage and expensive time off from work for the rider. .

Recovery:

Rob was treated for the injuries and participated in minimal physical therapy. He remained in a cast for two months and had limited use of his left hand. He has fully recovered and rides recreationally.

Rider:

Dave Auld, 31 year old male

Experience Level:

Pro class racer for 3 years

Description:

A very long run was planned that involved stopping and walking over two sections with cattle grates. Rocks were purposely left in the road to signal the approach to the first grate. The second grate was located just after the campground where the riders were staying.

The stop for the first grate went as planned. Afterward, however, the lead rider got out ahead by himself. He apparently missed the campground landmark and his planned shut down area. The rider attempted a hard stop after seeing the second grate. While still braking, the rider and luge crossed onto the grate about 10 mph. The wheels and rider's right foot went through the grating and caught.

Injury:

Fracture of the right distal fibula (broken ankle)

Analysis:

Although the rider may have attempted to stop braking and ride across the grate, it is very doubtful he would have made it across and may have sustained much worse injury. The sections on either side of the grate presented even greater hazards. Ultimately, the rider was not sufficiently familiar with the road to support the initial speed he was traveling. Although he knew the cattle grate was coming up, he was traveling too fast to stop by the time he saw it.

Recovery:

While still in his cast, Dave continued to ride along in the truck and encourage his teammates. After 3 months the cast was removed and in 6 months, Dave was racing again.

Rider:

Kelly Green, 32 year old male

Experience Level:

Pro class racer with 5 years experience

Description:

On the third run down a mountain highway, the rider gave his partner a few minutes head start. The three mile section snaked through a couple of micro-towns and then opened up into fast sweepers (60+ mph) before the run out.

He entered a sweeping left turn already on the outside white line. Unable to hold the turn, he drifted further into the dirt. He slid parallel to the road until he impacted a mileage marker, which broke off his footpegs and lodged under his left kneecap.

Injury:

Broken kneecap

Broken hip

Multiple foot fractures

Multiple pelvis fractures

Severed tendons in knee and hand

Internal bleeding

"Impressively" bruised testicles

Analysis:

The rider sighted a police car and found his thoughts wandering away from the immediacy of the road. Three turns prior to the accident he attempted to refocus on the road and remembers engaging in an internal dialog, "You better focus boy, and now."

He also credits the road with being deceptively fast. As with many roads with high speeds and sweeping turns, it seems easy until something goes wrong. Once a rider goes off onto a dirt shoulder, brakes are practically useless and the rider will slide a long way before coming off the board or impacting an obstacle.

The rider also believes his line into the turn was inappropriate given the sliding characteristics of the hard wheels he was running. It is particularly important to recognize that any equipment change will probably make the board handle poorly until it has been tuned for that particular set up. Unfortunately, many handling problems will not manifest until the rider is sliding in a fast turn; then all hell breaks loose.

His own comment on the predictability of the accident was "I had always thought that if I was going to get hurt luging it would be racing. WRONG . . . "

Recovery:

Kelly spent two weeks in the hospital and another twelve months with severely impaired mobility. He has two long screws in his hip; sixteen screws and three plates in his pelvis. He believes he has now reached max recovery with 80% of left knee function and 90% strength and flex on the left hip joint.

"I still love the sport" says Kelly, "I am working on a multisport magazine called 'speed&soul' that will include road luge as one of several key sports. I still longboard, but have retired from the luge."

Since his recovery, Kelly continues to spectate at Street Luge racing events and served as an IGSA Official at the '97 X Games.

Rider:

Tony Magno, 29 year old male

Experience Level:

Pro class racer for 1 year, previous FIGR Amateur Champion.

Description:

This racer was the Golden Boy of the amateur circuit. With sponsorship and a fan base, he was looking forward to a strong year of pro class competition. As the X Games Qualifier was only a month away, the rider decided to really focus his efforts, training on increasingly challenging roads.

Practicing with experienced pro class racers on their home hill, the rider had been warned that the hill was totally unforgiving of accidents. One of his hosts had crashed and broken both ankles only months earlier on a surprise decreasing radius.

On the first run down the hill, the pace slowed to 25 mph and the rider took the lead despite the sharp turns and treacherous cliffs. Unfortunately, he was surprised by the same decreasing radius and ended up going wide, sliding into a guard rail. Upon impact he attempted to pull his feet upward but his right leg was pinched between the luge handles and the metal railing. He glanced off the barrier and slid on the ground to a stop.

The riders leg was nearly cut off and remained attached by 1/4" flap of skin and muscles. One of the other riders had a cell phone in the chase car and called for an ambulance. Because of the severe bleeding, the ambulance that arrived called for an immediate evacuation by helicopter.

Injury:

Severe contusions

Compound fracture of tibia and fibula

Near amputation of the right lower leg

Severe blood loss

Analysis:

The rider had no business taking the lead on a pro class rider's home turf. Aside from ignoring etiquette issues, the rider took unnecessary risks by not allowing his hosts to point out braking zones for the dangerous areas. "Local Knowledge" will always lead you into a turn hotter that you would try it alone. And when the locals hit the brakes, you'd better be behind them.

Recovery:

An excellent surgeon was able to reattach Tony's leg. For several months, he continued to attend races in his wheelchair—A grim reminder of when things go wrong. Tony was advised that he may not ever be able to walk again, but he accelerated through physical therapy and was back to work in 6 months.

"I might try a fun run on the luge again some day," Tony said, "But I won't go near any mountain roads. I also won't ever race again. I satisfied that urge. To race competitively, you have to ride on the edge between bravery and innocence. Since the accident, I can no longer believe that the serious injuries happen only to the other guys. Sometimes the other guy is you."

Rider:

Daryl Thompson, 28 year old male

Experience Level:

Pro class racer for 2 years

Description:

The day after a rained-out competition at Lake Castaic, California, many of the racers gathered for a fun ride on the nearly deserted Templin highway. Unfortunately, the road was not *totally* deserted. Moving aggressively through a right sweeping turn, the rider was startled to see a vehicle coming up the road. Attempting to increase visibility, he sat up in the turn and was unable to hold the inside lane. Consequently, the board slid wide and he was caught on the wrong side of the road facing the oncoming truck.

Making the proper decision between impact with a moving vehicle and extending further to the outside corner, the rider chose the latter. He went off into the dirt and launched off an embankment at about 50 mph. He impacted, feet first, into the side of a dirt hill.

Injury:

Broken ankle

Broken leg

Analysis:

The rider found himself in the opposing lane, facing traffic, on an open road. Even when traffic conditions are extremely light, this position invites danger. Daryl believes he should have maintained his composure and held to the inside lane. A few of the riders present felt they would have negotiated the gap between the oncoming vehicle and the outside edge of the pavement. Nevertheless, the best analysis remains the strong advice: Stay on your own side when riding open roads.

Recovery:

Daryl healed adequately to qualify for and compete in the '97 X Games. He continues to race in the professional class and likes to be called "Lugenstein."

Rider:

Gary Moth, 27 year old male

Experience Level:

Pro class racer for 2 years

Description

At the '97 IGSA Open Qualifier, the racer was unable to hold his line through a turn and impacted a dense wall of hay bales around 50 mph. Because of his body position and speed during impact, a significant amount of force was transferred directly to the racer's legs.

Injury:

Two broken ankles.

Analysis:

The rider was into a set of turns faster than he was able to negotiate them. This was particularly common at this race, where the stakes were high (X Games qualifying slot) and the chicanes were severe. No racer at this event made it through the course without braking. Unfortunately, even the less experienced riders tried, sometimes with catastrophic results. Prospective racers are reminded that hay bales are not soft, and any deviance from a race course suggests injury.

Recovery:

After leaving the California hospital, Gary managed his way home to New York. Amazingly, he returned a month later to compete in the '97 X Games (with braces under his leathers).

Rider:

Bret Batchelor, 36 year old male

Experience Level:

Sport class racer for 1 year

Description:

This racer earned a slot at the X Games Open Qualifier by moderating his fabulous start with his inexperience at finding a way through the hay bale chicanes.

The '97 X Games coverage featured a quick segment of this orthopedic surgeon setting the broken leg of a patient, quickly followed by his own severe injury. During a qualifying run, the new racer exceeded his ability to negotiate the hay bale walls and found himself taking a line which led to a perpendicular impact with the set of bales defining the next turn.

Injury:

Compound fracture of the right leg.

Analysis:

The rider's incredible starting skill earned him a place in a professional field for which he may not have been ready. Many racers crash during qualifying by taking aggressive lines which sometimes don't pan out. This accident was exacerbated by this new racer's "target fixation" the moment he realized he would not cleanly make the turn. With more experience, he may have tried to slide sideways into the hay bales, greatly lessening the impact.

Recovery:

Bret's wife currently believes he is retired, although while spectating at a recent race he revealed he was waiting for her to forget about the injury so he could return to competition. Bret earned an unforgettable place in the racer's hearts through good sportsmanship, and by providing trackside medical attention when he wasn't demolishing the Amateur field.

Conclusion

I've written this book as a Survival Guide because I don't want you to get hurt or run afoul of the law. Almost every piece of advice is followed by a caveat. But if the sport were truly about injury and arrest, I wouldn't bother writing. I wouldn't even bother participating. Fortunately, street luge is about something altogether different.

In *Parachuting, the Skydiver's Handbook*, Dan Poynter writes, "If riding in a plane is flying, then riding in a boat is swimming. If you want to experience the element, get out of the vehicle." I suppose my adventures as a skydiver and professional scuba instructor were about getting out of the vehicle. Street luge is about getting out of the vehicle also.

Every time I slip into tight leathers and strap on a full face helmet, the road takes on a different look. I think it's the same for all of us. You never really notice pavement until you plan to do fifty, a quarter inch off the deck. Suddenly you're intimate.

And maybe that's the appeal. Becoming intimate with your surroundings. Perhaps our relentless pursuit of comfort has drained away normal experience. So we pursue other ways to keep in touch.

Regardless of car racing analogies, luge is not about controlling a high tech vehicle. Luge is about sliding your BODY along the surface of the planet. Sliding at a high velocity. We only need wheels because we slide on paved surfaces. The rest of our equipment keeps the wheels underneath us.

"Luge" is a French word meaning "sled." As a child I can remember sledding the snowy hills near our rented mountain cabin. The thrill was fabulous, but it never lasted long enough.

There is something in our nature which hungers for a long free ride. There is a special appeal to coasting. Perhaps it's the basic instinct which compels mankind to travel the globe. Like birds soaring the landscape on a thermal, we want to ride an endless wave throughout the endless summer.

Ski resorts exist to satisfy our adult need for longer snow runs. Street luge exists because asphalt extends even farther. The reason we do our sport is not the complicated balance between life affirmation and a death wish. It's really about taking a playground slide and extending it 14 miles down the side of Mount Whitney.

While not a "radical sport," street luge can supply a radical thrill. Particularly while you are learning. The first time you roll through 30 mph it seems like you'll accelerate right through the sound barrier. It's scary, it's thrilling, and it's fun. But every road has a terminal velocity and you quickly get comfortable with the journey to speed.

Street luge is more accurately classified as a "technical sport." Methodologies and equipment make what we do safer. They also allow us to try things we would never attempt without protection. Achievements in the technical sports come from establishing safe baselines and adventuring out from there. How else could we have worked up to 80 mph on a skateboard?

Even after you develop your skills and a particular road is no longer scary, riding the luge is still fun. Watching the world sail past the sides of your shoes is the finest sensation of travel. As you master the sport and become comfortable at speed, you'll appreciate the experience even more. Like the thrill of falling and the joy of a roller coaster, danger isn't requisite for fun. Changing G-forces and rushing wind have basic human appeal. In some small areas of our lives, it's nice we're so easy to please.

Index

2"x4" board 17, 27, 65, 170
60/40 ratio 61

A

ABEC 90
abrasions 22, 116
acceleration under full brakes
  121
acceptability 65
accidents 21, 31, 73, 123, 165
aero board 25–26
aerodynamic 30, 32–33, 42,
  43, 45, 46, 48, 49, 50, 53,
  60, 70–72, 101, 103, 130, 137,
  169, 184
affordability 79, 81, 92, 102,
  104, 106–108, 153
aluminum angle 55
Amos, Ron 56, 172, 173
animals 126
Ansted West Virginia 176
Army Surplus 103
Auld, Dave 65, 67, 71, 126, 199

B

Batchelor, Bret 181, 206
Bates Leathers™ 105
Baumea, Don 171
bearing shields 92
bearings 90–94, 156, 169
Bell Wedge™ 98
belly pan 42, 44, 50
bent axles 83, 94, 96
Bernstein, Zac 67, 196
bicycles 18-21, 54, 115, 117, 152,
  188
bike paths 126, 185

body angles 49–50
body English 138
body position 25, 205
Bonelli Park 174
Boston, Ding 177
bounce test 41
braking
  15, 30, 43, 85, 108, 118, 121, 123,
  129, 134-136, 138, 141, 144,
  155, 156, 163, 199, 205
braking area. *See* run out
British racers 177
Brown, Beau 171
Bullet Board 71, 72, 192
bumpers 28, 53, 71, 169
business parks 125
"Butt-Boarding" 17, 176

C

California Extreme Sports,
  TV show 13
carburetor cleaner 93, 113
catastrophic equipment failure
  41, 63, 64, 72, 81
catastrophic injury
  16, 22, 131, 164
cattle grate 115, 127
Cayer, Tim 194
Cazin, John 80
center of gravity 44
ceramic bearings 91–92
certified welder 72
chase car 112, 117–119, 153
children 21
city permits 171
cliffs 126
closed roads 19, 132
Coates, Guy 178

Order Form

Name _____

Address _____

City/State/Zip _____

Telephone _____

Please send me the following number of copies of
the *Street Luge Survival Guide* _____

I have enclosed a check or money order for:

$14.95 per copy	_____
Calif. residents add ($1.16) tax per copy	_____
Foreign orders add $2.00 per copy	_____
$3.00 Shipping	_____
Total Amount	_____

Mail Order Form to:

GRAVITY
PUBLISHING
POST OFFICE BOX 50037
Irvine, CA 92619-0037
www.GravityPublishing.com

Order Form

Name _____

Address _____

City/State/Zip _____

Telephone _____

Please send me the following number of copies of
the *Street Luge Survival Guide*   _____

I have enclosed a check or money order for:

$14.95 per copy   _____

Calif. residents add ($1.16) tax per copy   _____

Foreign orders add $2.00 per copy   _____

$3.00 Shipping   _____

Total Amount   _____

Mail Order Form to:

GRAVITY
PUBLISHING
POST OFFICE BOX 50037
Irvine, CA 92619-0037
www.GravityPublishing.com

Order Form

Name _____

Address _____

City/State/Zip _____

Telephone _____

Please send me the following number of copies of
the *Street Luge Survival Guide*   _____

I have enclosed a check or money order for:

$14.95 per copy	_____
Calif. residents add ($1.16) tax per copy	_____
Foreign orders add $2.00 per copy	_____
$3.00 Shipping	_____
Total Amount	_____

Mail Order Form to:

GRAVITY
PUBLISHING
POST OFFICE BOX 50037
Irvine, CA 92619-0037
www.GravityPublishing.com